WHOLEFOOD
FOR THE
WHOLE FAMILY

In the same series

How To Boil An Egg – Simple Cookery For One
An Indian Housewife's Recipe Book
The Microwave Planner
Microwave Cooking Properly Explained
Out Of The Freezer Into The Microwave
Food Processors Properly Explained
Slow Cooking Properly Explained
Pressure Cooking Properly Explained
Deep Freeze Secrets
Basic Freezer Recipes
Right Way To Make Jams

All uniform with this book

WHOLEFOOD

FOR THE

WHOLE FAMILY

by

Sue Scott

PAPERFRONTS
ELLIOT RIGHT WAY BOOKS
KINGSWOOD, SURREY, U.K.

Made and Printed in Great Britain by Hunt Barnard Printing Ltd., Aylesbury, Bucks.

CONTENTS

FOREWORD

Ten years ago our family's eating habits were the same as those of most other people. We were a family of four – Mum, Dad and two children.

My husband had a serious sleep problem, often only sleeping for two or three hours a night. His digestion wasn't wonderful either. I suffered from frequent migraines which had begun in my early school days, and arthritis which was causing me pain in my shoulders and hands. Our first daughter, then six years old, seemed fine but, later on, she too began to complain of headaches. Our first son, then three, was severely asthmatic and had screamed almost every night during his first two years!

Looking around us at other families we realised that, although we had had a few more than our fair share of problems from time to time, we certainly were not unusual. We were not and are not neurotic hypochondriacs either!

The medicines and inhalers prescibed for our son were not attacking the cause of his asthma; they were simply making him dozy and lethargic. The medicines I took were not curing my ailments either.

Things had to change.

We then learned of naturopathy which encourages healing naturally and without the use of drugs, by means of diet, water therapy and breathing exercises. We decided to try it with our asthmatic son and in so doing we embarked on a path which was to lead the whole family into the world of wholefoods.

The first step we took was to feed our son an ovo-vegetarian wholefood diet on the advice of the naturopath; that meant no more meat, fish, fowl or commercially processed foods. He was not allowed any sugars (not even honey) nor any milk products, nor was he allowed any stimulants such as tea, coffee or cocoa. Panic! What could I feed him on? To begin with, meals were a nightmare until I began to develop the recipes you will find later in this book.

Our son was only four at the time and passionately loved cheese on toast. However, the frequent severe asthma attacks he was experiencing frightened him so much that he tried really hard to stick to the rules. I kept him company and followed his diet whenever we ate together.

Although progress seemed slow and we could not feel sure until much later, we soon realised how very allergic he had become to certain foods, particularly to all milks and milk products.

Our second son was an easy baby but later showed slight signs of hyperactivity when his sleep became disturbed and his movements unusually jerky and erratic. A spilt drink at every meal was normal. Hyperactivity can be the result of a poor diet, high in preservative-laden "junk" foods. However this was not the cause of our son's hyperactive behaviour. He apparently could not tolerate too many foods which were high in natural salicylates. These are chemically like aspirin and are found in many natural foods, mainly in some fruits but also in almonds. Oranges were the worst culprits in our son's diet. Even eaten in small amounts, salicylates can affect behaviour in both children and adults. Simply cutting down on the quantity our son ate controlled his hyperactivity immediately. It was a most welcome discovery and one which was a direct result of our research into healthy eating.

Our second and third daughters joined our family when they were nine and eight years old respectively and brought with them health and behavioural problems. The elder one was suffering from severe asthma and eczema; the younger one from hyperactivity.

During their first few weeks with us I offered them the foods I thought they liked, but I soon realised that they preferred the wholefoods we enjoyed, particularly the fresh fruit and vegetables. By this time I had learnt a little more about nutrition but still found adapting recipes very difficult. However I was much helped in my task because the children were always willing to try out new foods or new combinations and have rarely been fussy at mealtimes.

Incidentally, there has always been one rule at our table.
The children are served a little of everything and expected to
eat it and, if they like it, they can always have more. Anyone
who shows signs of fussiness is simply sent away and not
offered anything else to eat until the next meal. They must
even miss any between-meal-treat that might otherwise
come their way. The rule may sound Victorian to some but it
has worked. All five young people eat heartily and
thoroughly enjoy their varied wholefood diet. They are
particularly fond of good Chinese and Indian food. Also,
through our emphasis on wholefoods, they have a better
understanding of what is good and what is bad for them.

Slowly during those early years, I introduced the family to
more new flavours and new textures. Six of us became
vegetarians – three lacto-vegetarians (those whose diet
includes dairy products) and three ovo-vegetarians (those
whose diet includes eggs but not dairy produce). The seventh
is almost vegetarian but he still enjoys fish occasionally.

Becoming a committed vegetarian wholefood family has
not always been easy. Friends and relations openly criticised
us and continually sowed seeds of doubt in our minds.
"You're depriving the children when they are with their
friends. They're only young." The children have indeed met
problems in school. Being different in any way is always
hard, but discussion at home has provided them with
powerful arguments!

Ten years on, my family will confirm that we are all the
better for becoming wholefooders and that we have neither
any doubts nor 90% of our former ailments. An added bonus
is that, as a result of improved concentration, school reports
are becoming a pleasure to read.

Our story is not so unusual nowadays as more families
take positive steps to a healthier lifestyle. We are no longer
considered cranky in the way wholefood vegetarians once
were. The moral arguments for giving up eating flesh, which
have naturally also played their part in our individual
decisions, have been reinforced by the case for good health, a
case which seems to us sufficient in itself. Our awareness that
we can be healthier without eating meat has been equally
important in how our lifestyle has changed.

Wholefood cookery can become a way of life. After plenty

of practice with my large family, I hope my collection of recipes will provide variety for everyone, whether you just want to dabble from time to time or you seek a continuing supply of new and nourishing recipes. None of my recipes will keep you tied to the kitchen for hours. Most will suit any occasion and I have specially included lots which are particularly useful for packed lunches and even camping.

For me, an interest in healthy natural wholefood eating and in properly balanced overall nutrition seem to be inseparable. I hope readers will spare a few moments on my opening chapters devoted to this aspect and that these together with the recipes themselves will help build up invaluable knowledge about healthier eating.

All of my family wish that our collection of favourite recipes will encourage you to try out new ideas of your own too. Our country's taste-buds have been overwhelmed by sugar, salt and other health-hazard additives for too long. We hope that others may grow to enjoy the real flavours and benefits of wholefoods as a result of our experiences and recipes published in this book.

Sue Scott

Note: Many readers may be aware that there are dangers in the incorrect use of fats and oils, and that beans need careful preparation. I would like to draw everyone's attention to Chapter 3 which, if followed carefully, should prevent any misadventures.

1

NUTRITIONAL FACTORS
TO CONSIDER

What are Wholefoods?
Wholefoods are natural foods which we eat in as near their
whole original form as is reasonable.

Why Wholefoods?
We are all familiar with the modern term *junk food*. Why has
it crept into our vocabulary?

During the last few decades people in the West have,
unknowingly, been taking part in a big dietary experiment.
The need to maximise farm production has led to the use of
vast quantities of chemicals, many of them suspected of
adversely affecting people's health. The risk these generate
for the consumer is extremely difficult to evaluate. In
addition, since the Industrial Revolution one of the main
commercial aims of the food industry has been to prolong
the *shelf life* of foods. Food quality has also suffered in the
interests of achieving ever more attractive presentation and
of providing the utmost user convenience. Gradually, with
increasing sophistication of techniques, more and more
additives and preservatives have infiltrated our diet and, at
the same time, much vital goodness has been *removed*.

Not all the changes have been bad. Food hygiene, for
example, has been greatly improved. However, how many of
us are in a position to recognise the degree of doctoring and
junk in the food we buy?

Thankfully, scientists involved in medical research and
many government agencies have at last begun to focus on the
dangers to health of such a refined, processed and chemical-
laden diet. Their research has shown links with allergies,
behavioural problems in young and old, and with degenerative diseases such as cancer, arthritis and of the heart.

Major reports published in Britain and elsewhere have focused public awareness on the facts and helped people to appreciate that, so very often where poor diet leads to disease, the accumulated problems only surface when it is too late to arrest them. Their findings in my view establish beyond reasonable doubt three things:

(1) being overweight, even mildly so, is dangerous;
(2) a high refined sugar intake, a high fat consumption (particularly saturated or animal fat) and a low fibre intake can each lead to ill-health;
(3) a good varied natural wholefood diet is not only healthy and energising, providing for all your needs, but can also play a significant part in curing, preventing and arresting disease.

My own family's commitment to wholefoods has been reinforced by these changes in medical and scientific understanding. For us, the improved health we have all enjoyed as a direct result of starting our wholefood diet has set the seal on the matter. The answer to my question "Why Wholefoods?" will be different for each reader. Assuming a shared desire to adapt to wholefood eating however, I will offer some of the reasons for doing so which seemed to me compelling, as well as some helpful suggestions. Then I will examine nutrients in more detail.

The quality of "fresh" food is often doubtful. Not only do our fruits and vegetables travel for days or even weeks, but they are grown in depleted soils with artificial fertilisers and are sprayed many times during their growing life, sometimes unnecessarily, with potentially harmful chemicals. Finally they are sprayed, waxed or packaged with further "unnatural" materials to preserve them. Organically grown produce, grown in naturally rich soil without any artificial fertilisers or pesticides, contains far greater amounts of vitamins and minerals. We choose it whenever possible.

We need to eat nutritious foods, especially those rich in calcium, magnesium, and vitamins C, E and A, to combat the pollution around us. Not only is most of our food polluted, but the air we breathe and the water we drink are often impure.

Refined, processed foods are largely stripped of vitamins

and minerals, causing deficiencies and deficiency-linked disease in those who eat them all the time. Scurvy was common when fruit and vegetables were absent in the diet in the past. Today, poor diet can be shown to be a factor in many more serious degenerative diseases. We are now becoming aware of the dietary connections with illnesses which take a long time to develop.

Such refined foods often contain salt and sugar. Although salt has been used as a preservative for a very long time, we consume it now, unknowingly, in a variety of foods, from ketchups to sweet biscuits. This can lead to excess. Salt is thought to be implicated in heart disease. Our sugar consumption is high for the same reason. It has become a vital ingredient in processed foods. A high intake of any sugar can be contributory in most of the degenerative diseases, and may be a cause of depression and of hyperactivity.

Many refined carbohydrates, white sugar and white flour for example, when eaten in varying amounts depending on the individual's tolerance, can cause unnatural results. They can alter mood and behaviour. They tend to raise the blood sugar level fairly rapidly, bringing feelings of well-being or excitement. The pancreas then has to pump out an abnormally large amount of insulin to lower that level which, in turn - while robbing the body of other essential nutrients, particularly the B vitamins   may produce tiredness, even depression and cravings for more of the same foods.

Individuals require a varying number of calories. This is dependent on many factors - lifestyle, height and weight, physical activity etc. Excessive consumption of carbo- hydrates, particularly highly refined "empty" carbohydrates, relative to excercise can lead to obesity which, in turn, can lead to ill-health.

Fats and oils present a major problem in the Western diet in which a taste for dairy products and fried foods, including snacks like potato crisps, has developed. The high con- sumption of animal fats and cholesterol in conjunction with a generally poor diet has become a hazard to health.

Most modern supermarket oils are refined and margarines are processed. They are therefore not as nutritious as the

seeds, nuts or beans from whence they came (see Chapter 3).
Margarines are generally made from vegetable oils which are
not only refined, but contain chemicals and preservatives.
Some margarines contain hydrogenated fat which may even
be harmful.

Butter, although a saturated fat (see p. 17), is a natural
product. There is some evidence that, unlike most other
animal fats, it may protect the heart.

However, the widespread use of antibiotics and growth
hormones on cattle has led consumers to question the value
of dairy products in their diet. Allergic reactions to milk
have become very common. The asthma, eczema and
headache sufferers in our family are definitely intolerant of
dairy products.

Raw, whole milk, although a saturated fat, is very
nutritious for those who are milk-tolerant. Natural, home-
made yoghurt is particularly nutritious when made from
unpasteurised goat, sheep or cows' milk.

The adulteration of meat and its high fat content seem
valid reasons for being as much of a vegetarian as possible.

It appears that one of the main secrets of health lies in
eating sufficient wholefoods containing plenty of roughage
and fibre to produce very soft, regular bowel movements.
Recent research points to constipation as one of the major
contributors to ill-health in the western world. Garlic,
brewer's yeast and foods high in vitamin C are natural
laxatives. Carob, a healthy alternative to chocolate, is also a
good bowel conditioner.

How can you achieve a Wholefood Diet?
An understanding of the nutrients required for a balanced
diet, plus variety and moderation, are essential ingredients in
a successful wholefood diet. However, eating is a social
activity too and it is almost impossible to stick to ideals all of
the time. Try therefore to avoid the following as much as
possible:

* sugars – all varieties except occasionally malt, rice syrup
  and a very little molasses
* white flour products
* packaged and processed foods

* added salt
* too much saturated fat (p. 17)
* high proportions of dairy produce;

and aim to:

* eat salads daily and include plenty of raw food in your diet
* eat "wholegrains": rice, cereals, bread, pasta
* sprinkle brewer's yeast and wheatgerm on cereals, fruits, in soups and gravies (p. 26)
* use locally grown produce
* select foods in season and organically grown (p. 12)
* look for free-range eggs, preferably from chickens fed on organically produced grain
* use only high quality, cold-pressed oils (p. 18)
* eat only when you are hungry, a little at a time, chew well and endeavour to stop eating before you feel full.

If questioned about your diet, always explain the reasons for altering it to ensure an enthusiastic response from others. Make changes slowly but do cut out all the worst possibly harmful additives immediately (see the appendix for a list of suspected carcinogens). Encourage everyone in the family to prepare new recipes and to modify old favourites.

UNDERSTANDING NUTRIENTS

We can broadly divide foods into macro-nutrients and micro-nutrients. Macro-nutrients are the visible bulky components such as carbohydrate, protein and fat, whereas the term micro-nutrients refers to the invisible parts, the vitamins, minerals and trace elements.

* A varied diet containing appropriate amounts from *all* food groups is essential to a healthy balanced diet.

Macro-nutrients

Carbohydrates
Carbohydrates are essentially the starches and sugars in our

diet. They are our natural sources of valuable fibre and a steady supply of energy. They require many vitamins, minerals and enzymes for their proper absorption. One gram of carbohydrate provides four calories; and at least 30g per day per person is recommended.

Among the best sources of good quality, easily digestible carbohydrate are "whole" grains, "whole" pastas, vegetables, fruits and natural sweeteners (see p. 28).

Grains: barley, brown rice (long and short grain), millet, wholewheat berries, buckwheat groats, oats, popcorn, rye, etc.

Pastas: wholewheat and buckwheat spaghetti, wholewheat macaroni, lasagne, shells and ribbons, Japanese noodles etc.

Legumes: aduki beans, blackeye beans, butter beans, chick peas, flageolets, haricot beans, kidney beans, lentils, mung beans, soya beans, split peas (p. 29, for bean preparation and cookery).

Proteins

Proteins are to be found almost everywhere in our bodies. They are often referred to as the building blocks of the diet, being responsible for growth and repair. They provide heat and energy if insufficient carbohydrates are available. Excess protein may be converted to fat in the liver.

* Only moderate amounts of protein are required in the diet of a healthy person.

Complete Protein

Proteins are broken down into amino acids during digestion. There are about twenty known amino acids, eight of which the body cannot make and these must therefore be found in food.

These eight essential amino acids are found together and in the correct proportions in all animal products – meat, fish, dairy produce, and in soya beans and soya bean products. These foods provide "complete" protein.

* Soya beans have been used as a staple food in the Far East for thousands of years but it is only within the last decade

that research in the West, mainly in America has proved
them to be such a valuable source of protein (equal to meat
in usable protein).

Tempeh, a fermented soya bean product, also contains
vitamin B_{12}, the vitamin which is most difficult to provide in
a vegetarian or vegan diet.

Incomplete Protein
Protein derived from non-animal sources is called "incomplete" protein. "Incomplete" proteins, eaten in small
amounts and at the same meal, combine together and
enhance each other, providing excellent "complete" protein.

A simple rule to follow is to eat a little from two or three of
the following four food groups at each meal: grains, seeds,
nuts and legumes (beans, peas, lentils etc.); sometimes using
dairy products too. The most widely used combinations are:

* grains (rice, wheat, maize etc.) and legumes (beans, peas,
  lentils etc.)
* grains and milk products
* seeds (sunflower, sesame, pumpkin etc.) and legumes.

Raw proteins are more valuable to the body as cooking can
partially destroy some of the essential amino acids. Sprouted
seeds, beans and grains are sources of superb protein (p. 30).

Fats and Oils
Fats are another source of energy but they take about eight
hours to be absorbed. (One gram of fat provides nine
calories.) Oils from vegetable sources in particular provide
us with the essential fatty acids that our bodies need but
cannot manufacture in sufficient quantities to provide for,
among other things, the production of certain hormones,
healthy cell membranes and healthy skin. Fats are also
required for the absorption of other nutrients including the
fat soluble vitamins.

Fats and oils can be roughly divided into two major
groups: *saturated fats* and *unsaturated fats*. Saturated fat is
solid at room temperature in a moderate climate and is
mostly of animal origin (one notable exception is coconut).
Unsaturated fat is of plant origin. Unsaturated fats can be

sub-divided into further groups, the most important of
which are *polyunsaturated* and *mono-unsaturated* fats.

Polyunsaturated fats, once extracted, remain liquid, even
when quite cool whereas mono-unsaturated fats will soli-
dify when slightly chilled.

* A diet based on "whole" grains, nuts and seeds, raw dairy
products (particularly yoghurt, cheese and milk from goats)
and eggs is well-balanced and should provide all the fats
required, some saturated and some unsaturated. However, a
little cold-pressed, unrefined vegetable oil, does change the
flavour of dishes and can be used instead of one of the above
sources or as a supplement if needed.

Cold-pressed oils have been extracted from the first or
second pressing of the seed, nut or bean and have had no
chemicals added to them. Only pure olive oil is strictly
"cold"-pressed. Others have been heated slightly in extrac-
tion but not harmed thereby. "Extra virgin" olive oil is the oil
obtained from the first pressing of the olive harvest.
Safflower, grapeseed, and sunflower are some of our
favourite cold-pressed highly polyunsaturated salad oils.
Unrefined, cold-pressed sesame oil, a mono-unsaturated oil,
is superb in pastry and wok cookery; and olive oil, the most
stable of all the unsaturated fats, is a delicious medium in
which to sauté vegetables and create Mediterranean dishes.

Cholesterol is to be found in every cell of the body,
particularly in the brain. The body manufactures sufficient
cholesterol to sustain life and health. Eggs are high in
cholesterol but they are a very balanced food as they contain
lecithin, a natural emulsifier which breaks down cholesterol.
As with any food, moderation is essential. Three or four eggs
per week from free-range, organically fed hens will do no
harm if the other sources of saturated fat in the weekly diet
are few.

Unsalted butter, a saturated fat, is fine if used sparingly by
those who are milk-tolerant. A commercial spread which is
free of preservatives, colour, whey and hydrogenated fat
would suit those who are milk-intolerant.

Ghee – clarified butter – is very safe for high temperature cooking, sautéing, lightly frying, roasting and for greasing baking trays. Those allergic to dairy products can usually tolerate ghee. (For recipe, see p. 35.)

* Certain fats are dangerous if used for high temperature cooking (p. 32).
* Variety is vital – too much of any one type of fat, even polyunsaturated fat, could lead to ill-health and obesity.

Micro-nutrients

These are the vitamins and minerals which are essential to life and health. Our understanding of their necessity is growing with research.

Whole grains, nuts, seeds, vegetables, grain and bean sprouts, fruits and a little dairy produce, brewer's and nutritional yeast, raw wheatgerm, seaweeds (particularly kelp) and cold-pressed unrefined oils are all valuable sources of vitamins and minerals.

* Organically grown produce contains far greater amounts of the micro-nutrients.
* Heating destroys many of the micro-nutrients in our food and a number of them depend on others for proper absorption.

Some Important Minerals and Vitamins and Where To Find Them

Calcium	sesame seeds, tahini (sesame seed paste), almonds, carob flour, sea vegetables, kale, broccoli, dandelion greens, molasses, sunflower seeds, soya beans, milk, milk products
Copper	whole grains, apricots, soya beans
Iodine	sea vegetables, kelp, garlic, onions, watercress

Iron	spirulina, prune juice, grains, apricots, brewer's yeast, bananas, raisins, millet, chick peas, blackstrap molasses, nuts, asparagus, oatmeal, pumpkin seeds, dates, spinach, lentils, egg yolks
Magnesium	green vegetables, whole grains, almonds, seeds, figs, molasses
Manganese	seeds, nuts, grains, leafy green vegetables, pineapple, kelp, egg yolk
Potassium	green leafy vegetables, whole grains, sesame and sunflower seeds, bananas, beans, oranges, molasses, milk
Selenium	wheatgerm, whole grains, broccoli, brewer's yeast, sesame seeds, garlic, milk products
Zinc	wheatgerm, pumpkin seeds, sunflower seeds, nutritional yeast, nuts, sprouted seeds and grains, wholewheat bread, whole oatmeal, brown rice, ground mustard, organically produced vegetables, eggs and raw milk
Vitamin A	yellow and deep green leafy vegetables (e.g. broccoli and spinach), beetroot, avocados, alfalfa sprouts, coloured vegetables (e.g. carrots and sweet potatoes), coloured fruits (e.g. apricots, peaches), milk and milk products, fish liver oil
Vitamin B (complex)	nutritional yeast, brewer's yeast, whole grains, molasses, leafy green vegetables, seeds, wheatgerm, nuts, malt, lentils, beans eggs and milk
Vitamin C	broccoli, green peppers, fresh organically grown vegetables and fruits, particularly berries. alfalfa sprouts

Vitamin D   (not found in vegetables or fruit), butter, eggs, fish

Vitamin E   fresh wheatgerm, cold-pressed unrefined oils, whole grains, green vegetables, nuts, eggs

Vitamin F
(the essential
fatty acids)   unrefined cold-pressed vegetable oils, nuts, seeds, nut and seed butters, butter

Vitamin K   alfalfa, green leafy vegetables, cauliflower, nuts, wheatgerm, egg yolk, yoghurt

Vitamin P
(C Complex,
Citrus Bio-
flavonoids,
Rutin,
Hesperidin)   buckwheat, grapes, pith of citrus fruits, peppers, cherries

2

THE WHOLEFOODER'S KITCHEN

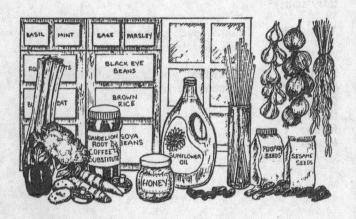

Foods for Your Store-Cupboard

agar-agar (setting agent)

apple juice concentrate and any other fruit juice
   concentrates available

arrowroot (thickening agent)

baking powder (make up from equal parts of arrowroot,
   cream of tartar and potassium bicarbonate; store in a
   screw-top jar)

beans – aduki beans, blackeye beans, butter beans, chick
   peas, flageolets, haricot beans, kidney beans, lentils,
   mung beans, soya beans, split peas (see also p. 30)

cereals – barley, brown rice, buckwheat, bulgar wheat,
   millet, oats, rye, wholewheat (organically grown wherever
   possible)

dried fruits – apricots, currants, figs, prunes, raisins, sultanas (unsulphured and either untreated or treated with vegetable oil and not with mineral oil)

dried mushrooms

dried yeast

drinks – Barleycup, dandelion root coffee substitute, herb teas, bottled fruit juices, bottled mineral waters

flavourings – capers, home-made chutneys/ketchups/pickles, miso, tahini, Tamari soy sauce, Vecon, yeast extract, sweet orange oil, grapefruit and lemon oil, pure vanilla

flours – brown rice, buckwheat, carob (a good cocoa substitute), chick pea or gram flour, maize, soya, wholewheat (all organically grown whenever possible)

herbs – basil, chervil, dill, fennel, marjoram, mint, oregano, parsley, rosemary, sage, tarragon, thyme

lactic acid pickles and juices

nuts – almonds, brazils, cashews, hazels, walnuts

cold-pressed oils – grapeseed, safflower, sunflower, sesame and "extra virgin" olive oil (p. 18)

olives – green and black

pasta – wholewheat lasagne, macaroni, rings, shells, spaghetti, tagliatelle, buckwheat spaghetti

peanut butter – free of sugar and salt if possible

rice – brown, long and short grain (organically grown if possible)

sea vegetables – arame, kelp, kombu, nori, wakame

seasonings – black peppercorns, cayenne, gomasio (1 part sea salt to 8 parts ground, roasted sesame seeds), mustard, paprika, sea salt (see also p. 25)

seeds – linseeds, pumpkin, sesame, sunflower

seeds for sprouting – aduki, alfalfa, chick, fenugreek, mung

soya milk powder

spices – allspice, cardamom, chillies, cinnamon, clove, coriander, cumin, garam masala, mace, mixed spice, nutmeg, root ginger, turmeric

spreads – sugar-free jams, pure honey, sunflower seed, tahini

supplementary foods – brewer's yeast, nutritional yeast, spirulina, kelp

tahini (sesame seed paste)

teas – chamomile, elderflower, lemon verbena, lime

flower, raspberry leaf, rosemary, sage
tofu, dried (soya bean curd)
tomato purée (always buy jars in preference to tins)
vinegars – brown rice, cider, herb-flavoured, white and
red wine vinegars

Fresh Foods For Your Fridge

breads – brown rice, fruity malt, 100% wholewheat
(organically grown wheat if possible), oat, pitta pockets
(p. 67), pumpernickel, rye

dairy produce – butter (unsalted), cheeses (vegetarian
cheddar, goats' cheese and quark – a hung yoghurt cheese),
eggs (free-range and from organically fed chickens if
available), milk (– raw milk may be better tolerated by
some people – goats' milk, freshly made soya milk)
yoghurt (goats', sheep's, soya, cows')

fresh fruit juices

fresh fruit and vegetables – ginger (fresh root), green leafy
vegetables, fresh herbs including plenty of garlic and
parsley, root vegetables, salad ingredients, sprouted seeds,
variety of fruit

other foods – *fresh tofu* (soya bean curd), store in water
in fridge, or in freezer without water and tightly sealed
       – *fresh yeast* (we buy a 1 kilo block at a time,
cut it into 1 oz (25g) pieces, wrap each individually in
greaseproof paper and store in a large freezer bag in the
freezer)

* Always choose fresh produce which is in season and
locally and organically grown or unsprayed if available.

* Always consider the packaging of foods when shopping –
some long-life cartons have an aluminium lining and this
could harm your health as aluminium is thought to be linked
with stomach disorders and memory loss.

Storing Wholefoods
Modern, centrally heated, warm homes are not ideal places
for wholefoods which are mostly sensitive to heat and light.
A cool larder or storeroom and a fridge are necessary. A
freezer is also useful.

Store *liquid sweeteners* in airtight jars – honey will keep
indefinitely, unrefrigerated, but fruit juice concentrates and
purées have a short life and must be refrigerated – date purée
will keep for a week or two, apple concentrate a month or
two once opened.

Home-baked wholefoods should be eaten within two or
three days and should be kept in airtight containers,
refrigerated or frozen. Frozen and thawed home-baked
wholefoods will keep a shorter time than unfrozen.

Grains, nuts and seeds must be stored in cool dry conditions
because of their oil content. In hot weather, refrigeration is
necessary. Cooked grains must always be refrigerated.

Cold-pressed oils should be kept in a cool place and out of
direct light – we keep ours on a shelf in a cool storeroom
(p. 32).

All dry goods should be stored in airtight containers in cool,
dry cupboards away from central heating boilers and pipes.

All fresh foods are best refrigerated, although eggs, cheese,
fruit, white cabbage and root crops keep well in a cool
storeroom where frost damage is not likely.

Seasonings
Here is a list of natural seasonings suitable for a healthy diet:

  herbs
  spices
  brewer's yeast powder and nutritional yeast
  spirulina, kelp and other seaweeds and sea plants
  Tamari sauce (pure soy)
  Shoyu soy sauce (soya and wheat)

miso (fermented soya bean paste)
wheatgerm
lemon juice

Salt need not be added to food if you live in a Western country where the climate is never very hot for any length of time. It is found naturally in vegetables, particularly the seaweeds and sea vegetables, and fruit. Adding extra salt is thought to over-stimulate the heart and is thus implicated in heart disease. Add a little lemon juice instead or use *kelp*, a seaweed high in iodine and a good source of calcium, or *spirulina*, a powder made from another sea plant and a rich source of vitamin B_{12}, iron and complete protein.

The enzymes in *miso* aid digestion but are killed at high temperatures – cool gravies, sauces, soups and casseroles slightly, before adding miso for extra salty flavour.

Brewer's yeast and nutritional yeast both add flavour to savoury dishes and are excellent sources of the B complex vitamins, protein and minerals. They can cause flatulence in those who are unaccustomed to them so introduce them slowly and in small quantities in drinks between meals for gradual acceptance!

Wheatgerm, if fresh and raw, adds flavour to cereals, yoghurts and fruit cups and is a great source of vitamin E, the vitamin most linked with a healthy heart (see Chapter 3 on warnings).

Herbs and Spices
Herbs and spices complement certain foods. Here are some suggestions.

Bean dishes	*herbs:* bay, basil, garlic, horseradish, lovage, marjoram, parsley, sage, savory, rosemary *spices:* cayenne, chilli, cumin, mace
Bread	*herbs:* garlic, lovage, parsley, poppy seeds *spices:* allspice, aniseed (anise), caraway, cinnamon, coriander

Cakes, Biscuits
herb: saffron
spices: aniseed (anise), allspice, caraway, cinnamon, cloves, coriander, ginger, nutmeg, vanilla

Curries
herbs: coriander leaves, garlic
spices: aniseed, allspice, cardamom, chilli, cinnamon, clove, coriander, cumin, fenugreek, ginger, mace, mustard, nutmeg, turmeric

Egg Dishes
herbs: basil, borage, capers, chervil, chives, dill, garlic, ginger, horseradish, marjoram, oregano, parsley, sage, savory, tarragon
spices: cayenne, paprika, vanilla

Fruits
herbs: orange flower water, sweet cicely
spices: allspice, cardamom, cinnamon, nutmeg

Grains
herbs: basil, garlic, lemon thyme, lovage, mint, marjoram, oregano, parsley, saffron, thyme
spice: cumin

Herb Butters
basil, garlic, parsley, tarragon, thyme

Milk Dishes
herb: bay
spices: cardamom, nutmeg

Pickles and Vinegars
herbs: dill, garlic, rosemary, tarragon, thyme

Salads
herbs: basil, borage, chervil, chives, dill weed, fennel root, lemon balm, lovage, mint, nasturtium leaves and flowers, parsley, rosemary, tarragon
spice: caraway

Salad Dressings
herbs: basil, chives, dill, garlic,

	marjoram, tarragon *spices:* cayenne, mustard
Sauces	*herbs:* sweet basil, capers, dill, garlic, horseradish, mint, parsley
Seed, Nut and Grain Loaves	*herbs:* basil, fennel root or seed, garlic, marjoram, parsley, rosemary, sage, thyme *spices:* cayenne
Soups	*herbs:* bay, garlic, parsley, rosemary, thyme
Stuffings	*herbs:* basil, fennel seed, garlic, lovage, parsley, sage, savory, lemon thyme, thyme, lemon rind
Vegetables	*herbs:* chervil, chives, dill, garlic, lovage, mint, parsley, savory, thyme *spices:* nutmeg, paprika

Some Vegetable and Herb and Spice Combinations

..... *artichokes with garlic and parsley butter*
..... *beetroot with orange and ginger*
..... *cabbage with caraway or ginger*
..... *carrots with bay or dill weed*
..... *cucumber with dill weed or mint*
..... *mushrooms with nutmeg or parsley*
..... *peas with mint*
..... *potatoes with dill, mint, nutmeg, paprika or parsley*
..... *swede with mace or nutmeg, nasturtium leaves and flowers, or black pepper*
..... *spinach with nutmeg or ginger*
..... *tomatoes with basil, chervil, garlic, mace, parsley, oregano, rosemary or thyme*

Sweeteners
Refined white sugar is not nutritious. I referred to its

deficiencies in Chapter 1. Nature gives us the sugar cane, and tribes who eat the cane in its "whole" state do not suffer from dental caries and the degenerative diseases common amongst refined sugar eaters. Brown sugar is as bad as white. Even the very dark brown unrefined sugars can only claim to contain minute traces of minerals. Some brown sugars are simply white sugars which have been dyed. If you must have sugar, use pure cane molasses as this does contain iron and calcium. But use only occasionally; too much, as in all things, can be bad for you.

Fresh and dried fruits†, sweet vegetables (like carrots and parsnips) and fresh fruit purées (apple and date particularly) are our first choices of alternative sweeteners as they retain the nutrients and fibre of the whole food.

Apple and other fruit juice concentrates† and fruit syrup (from stewed Hunza apricots, dates, prunes and figs) are suitable so long as their use is restricted. Maple syrup now and again is delicious on pancakes and in a meringue mixture, but as with the fruit concentrates, don't get "addicted"!

Raw honey is a mixture of glucose and fructose and is thought to have wonderful healing powers. It contains useful enzymes but these are killed if heated above the temperature of the hive (about 115°F/46°C) so choose to eat raw honey, preferably unfiltered, if you want the benefits. We love the "cappings" which are rich in pollen too.

Malt extract and rice syrup are other valuable nutritious sweeteners. They are grain sugars which are thought to be absorbed more slowly by the body, therefore supplying a slower and steadier source of energy than sucrose.

Carob flour and tahini (sesame seed paste) are useful sweeteners too, although less sweet than the others I have listed.

† Natural concentrated sweeteners and fruits, particularly dried, stick around the teeth and can become as much of a cause of dental caries as refined sugars.

Beans
Beans contain some problem-components; one is a trypsin

inhibitor which prevents digestion and another is phytic acid which binds up zinc and other minerals.

These must be destroyed either by cooking well or by sprouting.

Cooking Beans
Smaller beans, like blackeyes and the little green mung beans, can be cooked without soaking first, just like lentils, but I prepare most medium-sized and large beans as follows:

Stage 1: Rinse.
Soak overnight in fresh cold water, in a fridge in hot weather.
Throw away the soaking water as it contains indigestible starches and poisons.
Stage 2: Cook by boiling well in fresh water for 10 minutes and then simmering until soft but not mushy.

* Never add salt during this first cooking as this will toughen beans, but a strip of kombu (seaweed) added instead may make them more digestible.

* Store cooked beans in the freezer with or without their liquid.

* If you are using the beans without the water they were cooked in, you can keep it to use as stock in soups, sauces and gravies.

Sprouting Seeds, Beans and Grains
Try sprouting seeds, beans and grains for superb sources of protein and vast quantities of vitamins and minerals. Alfalfa seeds are among the easiest to experiment with if you are a beginner.

Stage 1: Put one or two tablespoonfuls of alfalfa seed in a jam jar, cover with fresh cold water and soak for three or four hours.
Stage 2: Secure a piece of muslin around the neck of the jar with a rubber band and strain the soaking water through it. (Small pieces of muslin can be purchased in cooking utensil shops.) Rinse and

drain again, leaving the jar tilted on the draining board so that the excess water can run off. (Sprouts will go mouldy if left too wet.)

Stage 3: Thereafter rinse and drain twice a day as in stage 2.

The sprouts will be ready to eat in two or three days, depending on the growing conditions. They can be grown in any well-ventilated position; a kitchen window-sill is ideal. Sprouters, which are like tiered seed trays, can be purchased in wholefood shops.

You can sprout almost any bean or seed – mung beans, chick peas, soya beans, sunflower seeds, lentils, wheat, oat groats, rye, unroasted buckwheat, barley etc. A pound of dried beans will yield about eight pounds of sprouts!

Utensils

We use mainly iron pans as they are about the best value for money, although iron does destroy vitamin C to some degree. If you buy iron pans, make sure they are not coated with plastic. Superior quality heavy stainless steel, porcelain-clad metal, or glass are more expensive but are safe.

As far as I am concerned a conventional oven is still the safest means of cooking. Microwave ovens are attractively promoted but there are still disagreements about safety aspects among researchers.

A garlic press, a vegetable steamer, a salad spinner for drying vegetables and a large wok are used every day in our kitchen, as is our one luxury – our food processor. This really saves time and is rapidly becoming a necessity, as it shreds the vegetables for salads and soups, grinds nuts and seeds for protein dishes, mixes cake batters, and takes the heavy work out of bread-making. Steaming vegetables or stir-frying them in a wok are the best cooking methods for conserving the most nutrients and colour. A wok requires very little oil. Stir-fried food should be eaten immediately, because despite being cooked in this way, food will still lose a lot of its goodness, and if left to cool, even more will be lost.

3

WARNINGS!

Oils

Refined oils (the type found in supermarkets) have usually been extracted from the seeds, nuts or beans with the use of chemicals, have been bleached and have had other chemicals added to them to prevent them from going rancid or foaming. We therefore only use cold-pressed oils. Different types of oils are explained on p. 17/18.

* Never eat rancid oils. Rancid oils are oils which have changed chemically and could be most harmful to health. If a white filmy deposit appears like wispy clouds in an oil, it is beginning to go rancid and should be thrown away. This deposit is not the same as the solid white droplets or mass which form when a saturated or mono-unsaturated fat is chilled, e.g. butter fat and olive oil.

* Keep all cold-pressed oils in a cool, dark place as they are heat- and light-sensitive and they change chemically when stored incorrectly.

* Never cook with highly polyunsaturated oils and fats at high temperatures. Highly polyunsaturated oils like grape-seed, safflower and sunflower oils become unstable when heated and could be very harmful to health. They are not suitable for frying or roasting, for example. We bake cakes with cold-pressed sunflower oil at gas 4 (180° C, 350° F) and pastry with cold-pressed sesame oil at gas 5 (190° C, 375° F). Cold-pressed sesame oil and olive oil are mono-unsaturated oils and are more stable than the polyunsaturated oils. All of these oils are far more nutritious when consumed raw (p. 18).

* Saturated fat may be used at a temperature above gas 5 (190° C, 375° F). Butter and clarified butter (ghee) or butter

oil (p. 18), are saturated fats and so they are our preferred medium for frying, roasts etc.

* Wheatgerm has a short life as the oil goes rancid very quickly. The wheatgerm darkens in colour and becomes bitter in flavour as it "goes off".

Beans
Beans must be prepared properly. They contain harmful elements in the raw state which include certain poisons, a trypsin inhibitor which prevents proper digestion, and phytic acid which binds up zinc and other minerals. These can all be destroyed by either soaking and cooking well or sprouting (p. 30).

Preparation Of Fruit And Vegetables
If you are forced to buy commercial produce, wash it thoroughly in a cider vinegar and water solution (1 tbsp of vinegar to 1 litre/1.75 pints of water). This will remove some of the toxic residue from sprays etc.

Utensils
Avoid using aluminium or non-stick coated pans as these could harm your health. Research is not conclusive but there is mounting evidence that aluminium stays in the cells of the body and the brain, and contributes to early memory loss, stomach upsets, headaches and blood pressure irregularities.
   Some non-stick coated pans may be dangerous if heated to a high temperature as the surface can be damaged.

* A natural way of making a non-stick surface is to apply some liquid lecithin to the pan. Lecithin is an oily substance extracted from soy beans, available in health stores in liquid and capsule form. Repeat the process each time you use the pan.

Food Wrapping Materials
Aluminium foil or cling film next to food is not advisable as there are questions surrounding their safety. Problems with aluminium were noted above. There is some evidence that wrapping fatty foods in certain types of cling films and sending microwaves through certain types of cling films may

both be harmful to health. Wrap food in a generous covering of grease-proof paper instead.

Waste disposal bags also often contain chemicals so should not be used to cover food.

RECIPE INFORMATION

Our advice to those new to wholefoods must be "Keep trying!" Recipes do not always turn out as they should, particularly if you are unfamiliar with some of the ingredients. One batch of 100% wholewheat flour will behave differently from another, depending on how absorbent it is. The newer strains of beans cook more quickly than older strains. Whole grains can be a little temperamental too. However, with a little practice, failures should become few and far between.

The recipes in the section on main courses have suggested accompanying dishes with each. These are intended to provide more ideas of combinations of ingredients and dishes, rather than specific recipes, although you will find many of them in this book.

Long preparation times will usually include long periods of inactivity on the part of the cook – we really don't spend hours preparing our meals but some planning is occasionally essential — e.g. 1 hour to cool in the fridge may be included.

Although we mention methods of keeping foods, eating them *fresh* is far more preferable from the point of view of nutrition. We always incorporate plenty of fresh raw foods at every "eating up" session of left-overs we may have to have!

Our ingredients' lists always suggest organically grown produce where appropriate (see also p. 12) but it may not be possible to obtain them in all areas. However, supply is fast responding to the increasing demand, so watch out for new growers in your locality or try growing your own. Many supermarkets now sell organically cultivated produce too. Your purse might not stretch to all organically grown ingredients, but I would suggest at least trying to have your *basic staple foods organically produced*, e.g. oats, rice, potatoes, carrots and bread.

Ghee (Clarified Butter) is used sparingly in most of the cooked main course recipes and for greasing baking trays.

How to make Ghee: Place 8 oz (225g) of unsalted butter in a saucepan and heat it gently until the butter boils. Lower the heat and, as the water evaporates, some milk solids will rise and some will sink. As those that come to the top thicken, scoop them off. When the butter oil left in the saucepan is clear, strain it through a sieve lined with a small piece of muslin. This is ghee. Kept in a covered earthenware dish or glass jar, unrefrigerated, it will not go rancid. (We keep ours next to the cooker with a small brush in it – an old pastry brush – ready for greasing pans etc.)

Measurements

The recipe measurements are given in imperial, metric and American cup measures. Follow one set of measurements only as they are not interchangeable. Where spoon measures are used they are all rounded spoonfuls for ingredients other than liquids. American cup measures are easy to use. Here are a few examples:

```
1 American cup = 8 fluid ounces or 225 millilitres
              = 1 oz (25g) chopped fresh herbs
              = 3 oz (85g) shredded coconut
              = 3 oz (85g) oats
              = 4 oz (110g) fresh breadcrumbs
              = 4 oz (110g) carob flour
              = 5 oz (140g) sunflower seeds
              = 5 oz (140g) chopped nuts
              = 6 oz (170g) wholewheat flour
              = 6 oz (170g) rice
              = 8 oz (225g) chopped onions
              = 8 oz (225g) dried beans, peas and lentils
              = 8 oz (225g) soft mashed butter
              = 10 oz (280g) peanut butter
```

In the recipes: tbsp = tablespoon; tsp = teaspoon; oz = ounce; lb = pound; g = gram; k = kilogram; pt = pint (20 fluid ounces); ml = millilitre; fl oz = fluid ounce.

4

BREAKFAST AND BRUNCH RECIPES

Breaking a night's fast is not always easy if you are only just out of bed, but it is a vital source of energy before school or work. We tend to reserve cooked breakfasts as weekend or holiday treats. For our weekday breakfasts we often have fresh fruit juice, home-made muesli, topped with fresh fruit and yoghurt (either soya or goats' milk yoghurt), wholewheat toast with a savoury or sugar-free spread and a herb tea.

My recipes for muesli and how to make yoghurt are at the start of this chapter. You will find wholewheat and other breads in Chapter 6, savoury and sugar-free spreads in Chapter 11 and ideas for alternatives to milk on pages 47–49. These can totally change the flavour of your breakfast cereals.

To build up heartier breakfasts or to transform the affair into "brunch" should the hour demand it, we tuck into alternatives or additional fare such as traditional porridge, chilled rice cereal, fresh fruit cream cereal, pancakes – brown rice, nutty, or fruity buckwheat pancakes perhaps topped with fruit and yoghurt, or dried fruit – corncakes, oat muffins, French toast, various cooked egg-based dishes, "mixed grills" e.g. "fried" bread with egg, tomato, mushrooms and home-made ketchup.

Recipes for all these ideas and more follow in the rest of this chapter except for home-made ketchup which can be found on p. 142.

Before coming to detailed recipes let us look at home-made yoghurt.

Yoghurt

Yoghurt can be made with goats' milk, soya milk, cows' milk or even sheep's milk. Each offers a different flavour. Sheep and goats' milk have a high fat content and their flavours become stronger with keeping but both can be successfully frozen.

Regular consumption of yoghurt many times a week maintains healthy intestines and thriving friendly bacteria. Be sure to increase your yoghurt consumption if you are taking antibiotics; they can kill these useful bacteria. Yoghurt is best when eaten raw, and is delicious plain or served with seasonal fresh or dried fruit and perhaps with sprinklings of chopped nuts, seeds, wheatgerm, oatgerm and brewer's or nutritional yeast. If you wish to add yoghurt to a very hot dish, stabilise the yoghurt first to avoid curdling, by beating in an egg or 1 tbsp wholewheat flour creamed with 1 tbsp water, before adding it to the dish.

One litre (1.76 pint) of milk will make sufficient yoghurt to fill four 12 oz (340g) jam jars. You need:

2 pt approx. (1 litre, 5 cups) milk (goat, soya, sheep, cow)
1 tbsp natural yoghurt to use as a "starter". (Once you have made your first yoghurt you can keep 1 tbsp of undisturbed yoghurt back to use as a starter for the next batch. For your first starter you can buy natural yoghurt; however, for making soya yoghurt I recommend you buy an entirely fresh starter every time. My best soya milk-based yoghurts have been made using natural sheep yoghurt as the starter.)
1 saucepan (not aluminium), sterilised by filling with boiling water and then emptying
1 sterilised spoon
1 sterilised bowl (optional)
4 sterilised jam jars, with their lids

1 Bring all the milk to the boil.
2 Leave to cool. Test after a while, by dipping in a clean finger. The correct heat at which to start making your yoghurt will be when you can comfortably hold your finger in, to the count of fifteen seconds or between 49°C (120°F) and 30°C (90°F). Then proceed.
3 Either put the yoghurt starter into the bowl and mix well with 1 tbsp of the warmed milk or simply add the yoghurt starter to all the milk, still in the saucepan.

4 Stir vigorously.
5 If using a bowl, return the mixture to the rest of the warmed milk and stir in well.
6 Pour into the 4 jars and screw on the lids.
7 Place the jars in a warm spot (in an airing cupboard or near a heater) for about 6 hours. The longer the yoghurt is incubated, the stronger and more acid the flavour will become.
8 Once set, store in a refrigerator; the yoghurt will keep well for 5–7 days.

* For a creamier yoghurt stir in 2 tbsp freeze-dried powdered milk at the beginning.

Fruit and Yoghurt Bowls

Seasonal fresh fruits, dried fruits or combinations of the two make a splendid start to any day. Serve topped with 1 tbsp fresh yoghurt, a few seeds such as pumpkin, sesame or sunflower, a few chopped nuts and a sprinkling of wheat or oatgerm.

Muesli

Home-made muesli is far more interesting than shop muesli; every bowlful is not only an exciting mystery but is extremely nutritious. Try to include oats frequently in your breakfast menus as their fibre content is most beneficial, and sprinkle a little wheatgerm on the top for added flavour and vitamin E.

Our basic muesli recipe per person is

    1 tbsp jumbo porridge oats (organic)
    1 tbsp jumbo barley flakes (organic)
    1 tbsp jumbo rye flakes (organic)
    1 tbsp millet flakes (organic)

but you can vary the combinations on different days. Soak all these flakes in about 5 fl oz (150ml, ⅔ cup) water or diluted fruit juice overnight. It is most important to do this in order to activate the enzymes which separate the protein and carbohydrate from the minerals, thereby producing a more digestible and more nutritious food. In the morning add

3-5 almonds, chopped
2 tsp sunflower seeds
2 tsp sesame seeds
1 piece of fresh fruit, chopped or grated

Serve topped with 1 tbsp of home-made yoghurt and a sprinkling of wheatgerm.

CEREALS

Our toppings can make cereals even more appetising – see also p. 45.

Oat Cream

(per person)

Soak overnight:

> 2 tbsp oats (organic) in 5 fl oz (150ml, ⅔ cup) apple juice or water

In the morning stir in:

> 1-2 tsp tahini (sesame seed paste)
> 3-5 almonds (ground or chopped)
> 1 piece of fruit (chopped or sliced)

Top with 1 tbsp yoghurt and a sprinkling of wheatgerm.

Cinnamon Oatmeal

(per person)

Soak overnight:

> 2 tbsp oats (organic) mixed with ½-1 tsp powdered cinnamon in about 5 fl oz (150ml, ⅔ cup) water

In the morning stir in ½-1 tsp freshly squeezed lemon juice and 1 tsp clear raw honey.

Hunza Rye Cream

(per person)

Soak overnight:

Hunza Rye Cream—contd.

2 tbsp jumbo rye flakes (organic)
1 tbsp jumbo oat flakes (organic)
5 Hunza apricots
7 fl oz (200ml, 1 cup approx.) water

In the morning stir in:

2 tsp pumpkin seeds
2 tsp chopped walnuts

Delicious served topped with fresh chilled yoghurt.

Cracked Groats
Preparation time 20 mins.   *(per person)*

2 tbsp oat grain (or other wholegrain: wheat, rye, barley,
or buckwheat - organic for preference)
1 tbsp sunflower seeds
ghee
7 fl oz (200ml, 1 cup, approx.) boiling water
1 tbsp tahini (optional)

Toast the grain and the seeds gently in a heavy pan lightly
greased with ghee, stirring almost continuously. Grind them
in a food processor or coffee grinder. Pour the boiling water
over this toasted and ground grain/seed mixture and stir
well. Simmer for 10–15 minutes until thick and creamy. Stir
in the tahini for extra creaminess and calcium. Serve topped
with a little hot fruit salad.

Bulgar Breakfast
Preparation time 15 mins.   *(per person)*

2 oz (55g, ⅓ cup) bulgar wheat
5 fl oz (150ml, ⅔ cup) boiling water
1 tsp concentrated orange juice (frozen)
2 tsp cashews, chopped
2 tsp sesame seeds
1 handful raisins or sultanas (unsulphured)

Put the bulgar wheat in a cereal bowl. Pour the boiling water over it and allow to stand for 10 minutes, or until the wheat has absorbed all the water and is light and fluffy. Stir in the fruit juice and add the nuts, sesame seeds and raisins. Serve topped with a little yoghurt.

Millet Porridge
Preparation time 30 mins.   *(3–4 servings)*
or about 2 hours if oven-cooked

> ghee
> 1 cup of millet to 2 cups of boiling water or milk
>   or
> 6 oz (170g, 1 cup) millet
> 1 pt 3 fl oz (650ml, 3 cups) boiling water or milk
>   (soya, goat, or other)
> nutmeg – for baking method

Method One
Lightly brush a warmed, heavy pan with a little ghee. Add the millet and toast it gently. Pour the water or milk over the millet, turn the heat to low and cover the pan with a well-fitting lid. Cook until the millet is soft, about 20 minutes, adding more liquid if required. Serve piping hot with stewed apples and a little nut cream.

Method Two
Alternatively, toast the millet as above, then transfer the toasted millet and liquid into a greased oven-proof dish, add an extra 2 cups of boiling liquid, sprinkle a little nutmeg on the top and cook slowly like a rice pudding (gas 1, 140°C, 275°F) for about 2 hours. Delicious hot or cold as a breakfast cereal or as a pudding with fresh fruit salad or stewed fruit.

Fruit Kasha
Preparation time 20 mins.   *(per person)*

> ghee
> 2 tbsp buckwheat (roasted)

Fruit Kasha—contd.

4 fl oz (110ml, ½ cup) water
1 tbsp goat yoghurt
1 pear (sliced)
wheatgerm
a sprig of mint or lemon balm

Warm a pan and lightly grease it with a little ghee. Add the buckwheat and toast gently for 2 minutes. Add the water. Bring to the boil, and cover the pan with a well-fitting lid wrapped in a clean tea-towel (this absorbs some of the moisture, but it must be tightly secured so that it cannot flap down creating a fire risk). Lower the heat to almost "off". Leave to cook slowly for 15 minutes. The buckwheat should be dry and light when cooked. Stir in the yoghurt. Pour the mixture into a small cereal bowl and arrange the pear slices on the top. Garnish with a sprinkling of wheatgerm and a sprig of fresh mint or lemon balm and serve.

Hawaiian Cereal
Preparation time overnight and 3 mins.   *(per person)*

2 tbsp cooked rice
1 tbsp oats (organic)
2 tbsp pineapple juice
2 tbsp water
½ banana (sliced)
5 almonds (chopped)
1 tbsp apple purée
unsweetened toasted coconut and oatgerm

Soak the rice and oats in the pineapple juice and water overnight in the refrigerator. In the morning stir in the banana and almonds and top with the apple purée and a sprinkling of coconut and oatgerm.

Apple Crisps
                              (fills a large glass storage jar)
Preparation time about 50 mins.

1 lb (450g, 3 cups) maizemeal or medium cornmeal

1 pt (550ml, 2½ cups) pure apple juice
pinch of cinnamon
cold-pressed corn oil for greasing the baking trays

Preheat oven at gas 2 (150°C, 300°F). Combine the maize-meal, apple juice and cinnamon together and blend well in a liquidiser. Oil 6 baking trays or Swiss roll tins with a little cold-pressed corn oil and divide the mixture equally between them, making a very thin covering. Bake for 45 minutes or until crisp and golden. When sufficiently cool to handle, crumble into small flakes and leave so that it cools thoroughly. Store in a glass, airtight container. Serve with chopped dried fruit and yoghurt.

Fat-Free Granola

(fills 2 large glass storage jars)

Preparation time 25 mins.

2–4 heaped tbsp malt (warmed)
1 lb (450g, 4 cups) approx. jumbo oats (organic)
ghee for greasing the trays

Preheat the oven at gas 5 (190°C, 375°F). Warm the malt in a large saucepan until runny in consistency. Stir in sufficient oats to cover lightly with malt and mix thoroughly. Spread this mixture thinly on 3 greased Swiss roll tins, and bake for 15 minutes. Fork over the mixture from time to time to prevent burning. The mixture will still be sticky when you take it out of the oven but the malt will harden as it cools. When thoroughly cool, turn into an airtight container. Keeps well for 2–3 weeks.

Add any fresh or dried fruit of your choice together with nuts and seeds when serving as a cereal or simply dip into the plain granola when feeling peckish!

Campers' Pan-Roasted Granola

Preparation time 10 mins.   *(serves 6–8)*

7 oz (200g, 2 cups) oats (organic)
3 tbsp raw wheatgerm
5 oz (140g, 1 cup) sunflower seeds
handful of dried fruit and nuts

Heat an ungreased heavy-bottomed pan and add the oats, wheatgerm and seeds. Toast them together over a medium heat for about 10 minutes, stirring them several times. Allow to cool. Add a handful of dried fruit, and nuts of your choice and serve with a yoghurt, milk or fruit juice.

* Alternatively try toasting wheat flakes (or other) with coarsely chopped hazelnuts on baking trays in a hot oven (gas 5, 190°C, 375°F) for 10–15 minutes.

PANCAKES

* Our pancakes are all delicious hot or cold with sweet or savoury spreads or toppings (see pages 45, 164 and 53) and are ideal for lunch boxes.

Rice Pancakes
Preparation time 15 mins.   *(10 small pancakes)*

   6 oz (170g, 1½ cups) brown rice flour (organic)
   2 tbsp fresh, raw wheat- or oatgerm (organic)
   1 tsp baking powder (p. 146)
   2 eggs, free-range and organically produced
   14 fl oz (400ml, 1¾ cups) water
   ghee

Combine the flour, wheat- or oatgerm and baking powder. Beat the eggs and the water together and then add to the dry ingredients to make your batter. Beat well. Heat a small heavy and preferably iron frying pan, 4″/10cm in diameter and grease lightly with ghee. Pour 3 tablespoonfuls of the batter into the pan and cook on a medium-high heat until the batter bubbles. Turn and cook the other side.

Buckwheat Pancakes
Preparation time 15 mins.   *(6 8 small pancakes)*

   4 oz (110g, 1 cup) buckwheat flour

8 fl oz (225ml, 1 cup) water
ghee

Combine the flour and water and mix well into a batter.
Heat a small heavy frying pan (4″/10cm in diameter) and
grease it lightly with ghee. Drop two tablespoonfuls of the
batter into the pan and cook over a moderate heat until the
pancake lifts away from the side of the pan. Turn over and
brown the other side.

Gram (Chick Pea) Flour Pancakes
Preparation time 15 mins.   *(6–8 small pancakes)*

4 oz (110g, 1 cup) gram flour
8 fl oz (225ml, 1 cup) water
2 tbsp goat yoghurt or curdled goat milk
ghee

Combine all the ingredients together to make a batter. Heat
a small, heavy pan (4″/10cm in diameter) and grease it
lightly with a little ghee. Pour three tablespoonfuls of the
batter into the pan and cook over a moderate heat until the
sides of the pancake lift. Turn and brown the other side.

TOPPINGS

These recipes for toppings make good spreads too. Multiple
quantities can be kept in small covered containers in the
freezer or in sterilised sealed jam jars. As with all sugar-free
spreads these must be refrigerated when opened and in use.

Strawberry and Apple Topping
(fills 1 × 12 oz/340g jam jar)
Preparation time 25 mins.

2 large, sharp, eating apples
4 oz (110g, 1 cup) strawberries
grated rinds of an organic or unsprayed orange and lemon

Strawberry and Apple Topping—contd.

**8 fl oz (225ml, 1 cup) orange juice including the
  freshly squeezed juice from the orange and lemon
pinch of cinnamon**

Wash and core the apples, peel only if you suspect they have
been sprayed. Hull the strawberries and wash if not organic
(p. 33). Put the strawberries in a saucepan and grate in the
apples. Add the remaining ingredients and bring to the boil.
Stir occasionally. Simmer for 10 to 15 minutes or until as
thick as you like it.

Dried Fruit Topping

(fills 1 2 × 12 oz/340g jam jars)
Preparation time 8 10 hours (overnight)

**1 cup dried fruit, any or mixed
1 cup water
juice and rind of an unsprayed or organic lemon**

Wash the fruit thoroughly. Soak overnight in the water with
the lemon juice and rind. In the morning process or blend to
a pulp and serve. Heat if you wish.

Spiced Pineapple Topping

This is a favourite of ours made as above with the addition
of 1 orange to every 4 oz (110g, 1 cup) dried pineapple and 1
tsp ground cardamom seed.

Treacly Sauce

Preparation time 15 mins.   (fills 1 × 12 oz/340g jam jar)

**2 oz (55g, ⅓ cup) raisins
8 fl oz (225ml, 1 cup) water
1 tbsp molasses
pinch of cinnamon
1 tsp arrowroot mixed to a paste with 1 tsp water**

Wash the raisins and put them into a saucepan with the

water, molasses and cinnamon. Bring to the boil, reduce the heat and simmer for 5 minutes. Add the arrowroot paste and stir continuously until the sauce thickens. Delicious served piping hot on pancakes garnished with a wedge of lemon. Alternatively cool thoroughly and store in a cool place in a screw-top jar.

Fruit and Yoghurt Topping

1 part fresh soft fruit: 1 part yoghurt

Wash and prepare the fruit according to instructions on p. 33. My basic yoghurt recipe is on p. 37. Simply process or purée the fruit and yoghurt together adding a little honey or maple syrup if wished.

More ideas for cereal toppings
..... Banana fluff – blend a ripe banana and ½ tsp lemon juice together in a blender or food processor. Makes 2 servings.
..... Soaked pumpkin seeds and/or sunflower seeds – soak 1 tbsp seeds overnight in enough water to cover them. Drain before topping cereal with them. Makes 2 servings.
..... Toasted sesame seeds – heat and lightly grease a heavy pan. Add 1 tbsp sesame seeds per person and toast lightly, stirring all the time. The seeds will pop as they cook.
..... Variety of dried fruits – in particular apricots and raisins (high in iron) and figs (high in calcium), unsoaked or soaked (wash and then soak dried fruits in water overnight and add both fruit and the soaking liquid to your cereal).

ALTERNATIVE MILKS

These make a pleasant and nutritious change to sheep or cows' milk in cereals, desserts and sauces. They are easy to prepare in a blender or food processor.

Soya Milk

Soya milk is an alternative to cows' milk which is very easy and inexpensive to make. One pound (450g) of soya beans will make up to a gallon (4½ litres) of soya milk.
Preparation time overnight and 40 mins.

> 1 lb (450g, 2½ cups) soya beans
> 2 pt (1.1 litres, 5 cups) water (for soaking)
> 2 pt (1.1 litres, 5 cups or more) boiling water
> vanilla pod

Rinse the beans and soak them overnight. Throw away the soaking water. Grind the beans finely in a processor or liquidiser with the boiling water. Use 1 cup of beans to 2 or 3 cups of boiling water depending on the strength of the milk required. If you plan to make yoghurt (see p. 37) from this milk then 1 part beans to 2 parts water is the better ratio. Transfer the mixture to a large saucepan. Add the vanilla pod, bring to the boil, lower the heat to simmering point and cook for 20 minutes. Stir occasionally.

A word of warning! Soya milk boils over easily and will also burn easily just like cows' milk.

When thoroughly cooked, strain the mixture through a sieve lined with a piece of muslin. Pour a little more hot water through the remaining soya pulp to rinse out any milk that might be left and squeeze well when sufficiently cool to handle (the drier the better as you will want to use the dry pulp in savoury dishes and desserts). Cool the milk and refrigerate or freeze it. Home-made soya milk will keep three to four days in the fridge and will freeze.

Soya milk lacks vitamin B_{12} but it can be fortified by adding yeast and molasses. For each ½ gallon (2¼ litres) add 1 tbsp nutritional yeast, 1 tbsp blackstrap molasses and 1 tsp vitamin B_{12} supplement. Blend as above.

Nut Milk

(makes ½ litre/18 fl oz approx.)
Preparation time overnight and 5 mins.

> 4 oz (110g, 1 cup) almonds or cashews, or half and half

almonds and sesame seeds
1 pt 4 fl oz (675ml, 3 cups) pure filtered or bottled water
optional sweeteners: 1 tsp molasses or 1 tbsp maple syrup

Soak the nuts or nut and seed mixture in the water
overnight (it is not necessary to remove the skins of the
almonds). In the morning, blend them well together in a
liquidiser with a sweetener, if desired, and then strain
through a sieve lined with a piece of muslin. Use the ground
nuts or seeds themselves in your breakfast cereal.

Tahini Milk
Preparation time 3 mins. (makes ½ litre/18 fl oz approx.)

3 tbsp tahini
16 fl oz (450ml, 2 cups) water
2 tsp clear raw honey
1 tbsp vanilla extract (p. 147)

Blend all the ingredients together in a blender or food
processor.

Fortified Goats' Milk
As goats' milk lacks folic acid, one of the B vitamins, it is best
fortified, particularly for young children. Blend 4 pints (2¼
litres, 10 cups) goats' milk with 1 tbsp brewer's yeast and
1 tbsp blackstrap molasses.

EGG IDEAS

We enjoy eggs cooked in many ways. We use free-range eggs
from organically fed hens.

* The cooking times for egg dishes will vary as everything
depends on the age and size of the egg – a very fresh egg
always takes a little longer to cook.

Poached – we half fill a shallow pan with water, bring the water to the boil, break in 1 egg per person, lower or turn off the heat, cover and leave to set for about 4 minutes. If you are cooking by electricity, half fill your pan with water which has been boiled in a kettle and then cook on a very low heat.

Boiled – we put our eggs into cold water, bring the water to the boil, lower the heat to a gentle bubbling and cook for 4 minutes. Test to see whether the eggs are sufficiently cooked by lifting one out of the water on a spoon and if the shell immediately begins to dry slowly then they are soft-boiled. If they dry rapidly they are hard.

Baked – we place an egg yolk per person in individual ramekins (custard cups) greased with ghee. Preheat the oven at gas 4 (180°C, 350°F). Spoon a little ghee onto each yolk. Whisk the egg whites until stiff, fold in chopped parsley and seasoning and whisk for a minute longer – the whites should form peaks – and then drop a large spoonful of white onto each yolk and spread gently to the edges of the dish. Bake for 5 - 10 minutes or until the white is golden in colour.

"Fried" – really pan-baked. We heat a heavy frying pan, grease it lightly with ghee and break in 1 egg per person. Cover the pan and cook for 3-5 minutes until the yolk has a white coating and the egg white is firm.

"Fried" Bread can be prepared as in the above recipe, browning both sides of slices of wholewheat or other whole grain bread. Pan-baked bread, eggs and a variety of vegetables, (e.g. mushrooms and tomatoes) make a healthy "mixed grill"

More Family Favourites, served with tomato ketchup (p. 142)

* Try carefully cutting a circle the size of an egg yolk out of a slice of wholewheat bread per person and putting the circles aside to toast or to use as breadcrumbs. Then "fry" one or two of the "holed" pieces of bread so that it browns on one side. Turn over. Break an egg into each hole, cover the pan

and leave to cook for 3–5 minutes or until the egg yolk has a
white coating and is cooked.

* · Alternatively, coarsely fork or chop ½–¾ of a cooked
potato per person, fry and brown lightly, and then make an
indentation for each of as many eggs as you wish to cook.
Break the eggs into them and "fry" as above.

Half and Half Scramble   *(serves 6)*

  8 oz (225g) firm tofu, grated
  6 eggs
  2 fl oz (55ml, ¼ cup) water
  1 tsp ghee or liquid lecithin
  seasoning – freshly ground black pepper or nutmeg

Grate the tofu. Whisk the eggs. Combine the tofu and eggs
with the water. Brush the bottom of a saucepan with a little
ghee or lecithin. Put the pan on the heat and pour in the egg
mixture. Add the seasoning and stir until the mixture
thickens to the desired consistency; for us that is not too wet
and not too dry.

French Toast
                                             (serves 4)

  3 eggs
  3 fl oz (75ml, ⅓ cup) milk of choice
  seasoning – pinch of nutmeg, pepper or a little vanilla
  ghee
  8 slices of whole grain bread
      (wheat, rye, mixed grains)

Beat the eggs, milk and seasoning together. Heat a heavy
frying pan and grease it with ghee. Dip the bread into the egg
mixture and brown on both sides in the hot pan. Delicious
served with home-made tomato ketchup (p. 142) or a
pancake topping (p. 45).

5

LIGHT MIDDAY MEALS
AND PACKED LUNCHES

Our bodies require good quality well-balanced fuel and so the midday meal, whether light or more substantial, must supply lasting energy. A tasty protein dish with an interesting salad plus a nutritious dessert and a "real" drink will do just that.

We have found that young children appreciate surprises and variety. They enjoy sandwiches cut in different shapes, and a selection of dip-sticks with a tasty dip is always very popular.

Older children and adults prefer pizzas, quiches, chilled omelettes or cold left-overs from the previous evening's meal with a salad, dessert and fresh fruit.

This book is designed for you to select dishes from different chapters to make up light lunches, picnics or whatever with ease. In this chapter and the next you will find dips and spreads and a wide selection of breads, pizzas and muffins. There are also pastries for flans, quiches etc. in Chapter 6. Salads have a whole chapter to themselves, p. 72, as do soups, Chapter 8, p. 93. To follow, you could choose a

sweet treat from Chapter 13, p. 176, or a cake or dessert from
Chapter 11, p. 146 and you could include a drink with a
difference from Chapter 12, p. 171.

SNACK-TIME

Tiding over the pangs of hunger between meals with a
nutritious snack is essential if blood sugar levels are to be
maintained and everyone kept more even-tempered! Children
can become fussy and difficult eaters if they are made to wait
too long on an empty stomach before meals. Our favourite
snacks are sticks and dips, fruit and nuts, seeds and
sweetmeats.

The recipes in the first part of this chapter are
interchangeable – the spreads make tasty dips and vice versa.

DIP-STICKS

Serve florets, wedges and sticks of raw vegetables with a
small bowl of dip; raw or lightly steamed carrot and turnip
sticks; cucumber and celery sticks; red radishes and white
mooli radish; raw broccoli and cauliflower florets; raw and
steamed green beans; strips of raw green and red peppers;
raw mushrooms; lightly steamed asparagus; cold, steamed,
small, new potatoes. Bread and pastry sticks and crispbreads
made from left-over dough are fun too (p. 69, 71).

SAVOURY DIPS AND SPREADS
Lemon Dip
(fills 1 × 12 oz/340g jam jar)
Preparation time overnight and 1¼ hours

  4 oz (110g, ¾ cup) chick peas (uncooked)
  1 pt 4 fl oz (650ml, 3 cups) water (for soaking)
  1 pt 4 fl oz (650ml, 3 cups) water (for cooking)

Lemon Dip—contd.

1 whole lemon, if organic (citrus fruits are heavily treated
   with chemicals) or just the juice if not
1 clove of garlic (crushed)
2 tbsp tahini
2 tbsp sesame seeds (toasted in a hot, very lightly
   greased pan)

Soak the chick peas overnight. Throw away the soaking
water and put the chick peas in a saucepan. Cover them with
fresh water and bring them to the boil. Cook rapidly for 10
minutes and then reduce the heat and simmer until soft but
not mushy, about 50 minutes. Process finely the lemon first
and then the chick peas. Combine together with the
remaining ingredients. Serve chilled. Keeps in a sealed
container in the fridge for about 3 days and may also be
frozen.

Hummus

Hummus is a Middle Eastern dish which can be a thin and
creamy dip, a thicker spread or, served with falafels (p. 136),
a nutritious and inexpensive main meal. Delicious hot or
cold.

Preparation time 5 mins.   *(4 servings)*

6 oz (170g, 1 cup) cooked chick peas (see previous
   recipe)
6 tbsp liquid used in cooking the chick peas
3-4 tbsp lemon juice
1-2 cloves of garlic, crushed
2 tbsp tahini

Grind or mash the cooked chick peas and blend them with all
the other ingredients either in a food processor or liquidiser.
Keeps well, refrigerated, for about 3 days and will freeze.

Crunchy Dill Dip

Preparation time 5 mins.   *(fills 1 × 12 oz/340g jam jar)*

8 oz (225g, 1 cup) crumbled firm tofu

1 tbsp cider vinegar
½ tsp mustard
½ tsp brewer's yeast or 2 tsp nutritional yeast
¼ tsp kelp
½ cucumber (chopped)
2 carrots (chopped)
½–1 tsp dill weed

Blend the tofu in a food processor or liquidiser with the cider vinegar, mustard, yeast and kelp. Add the remaining ingredients and stir well. Use within 3 days.

Avocado Dip

(fills 1 × 12 oz/340g jam jar)
Preparation time 5 mins. plus time for chilling

1 large ripe avocado
4 oz (110g, ½ cup) soft tofu
½–1 clove of garlic, crushed
juice of ½ lemon
¼ tsp cayenne pepper

Remove the stone from the avocado and scoop out the flesh. Blend the flesh with the other ingredients and chill well. Place the avocado stone in the jar or serving dish with the dip to prevent discoloration. Keeps up to 24 hours if refrigerated.

Crunchy Nut Butter

Preparation time 5 mins.   *(fills 1 × 12 oz/340g jam jar)*

4 oz (110g, ½ cup) tofu
2 tbsp peanut butter
1 tsp lemon juice
4 small sticks of celery (chopped)
water to thin mixture if necessary

Blend the first three ingredients together and then stir in the chopped celery. Keep for 2 3 days, refrigerated.

Curry Dip
Preparation time 5 mins.   *(fills 1 × 12 oz/340g jam jar)*

4 oz (110g, ½ cup) tofu
1 tbsp tahini (optional)
½–1 clove of garlic
juice of ½ a lemon
1 tsp curry powder
1 tbsp sultanas

Blend the first four (or five) ingredients until smooth. Stir in the sultanas. Keeps for 2–3 days, refrigerated.

Cashew Dip

(dip for 2–4 people)

Preparation time overnight and 5 mins.

2 oz (55g, ½ cup) cashews
3 fl oz (100ml, ½ cup) water
½ garlic clove
1 tsp lemon juice

Soak the nuts in the water overnight. Next day, crush the garlic and process the nuts, water and lemon juice together into a cream. Add the garlic and stir well.

For a smoother dip, add 1 tbsp cold-pressed sunflower oil and increase the lemon juice by 1 tsp when processing. This also makes a delicious salad dressing. Keeps for 2 days in a covered container in the fridge.

Egg and Veg Spread
Preparation time 5 mins.   *(fills 1 × 12 oz/340g jam jar)*

2 hard-boiled eggs
2 spring onions, chopped
2 tbsp chopped nuts – almonds, walnuts
2 tbsp chopped celery
2 tbsp steamed broccoli
water to add if mixture is too dry
seasoning: black pepper

Combine all the ingredients together and process to make a spread. Alternatively chop all the ingredients and toss them together to provide a crunchy filling for pitta pockets (p. 67).

Barbecue Spread

This recipe illustrates how simple it is to create a sandwich filler out of the previous evening's left-overs. Vegetarian dishes seem particularly easy to transform the next morning with the help of a food processor and an odd tablespoonful of either tahini, cold-pressed oil or even water.

Preparation time 5 mins.   *(fills 1 × 12 oz/340 g jar)*

   2 tbsp cooked millet
   2 oz (55g, ¼ cup) crumbled firm tofu
   2 tbsp grated celeriac or carrot
   1 tbsp home-made spicy tomato sauce (p. 143)
   1 tsp Tamari soy sauce
   water if necessary

Process all the ingredients together in a food processor or blender to form a smooth spread. Use same day.

Lentil Spread
Preparation time 5 mins.   *(fills 2 × 12 oz/340g jars)*

   4 oz (110g, ½ cup) cooked red lentils (p. 30)
   4 oz (110g, 1 cup) fresh wholewheat breadcrumbs
   1 tbsp tomato purée mixed into 2 tbsp water
   1–2 tsp Tamari soy sauce
   1 clove of garlic, crushed
   2 tsp dried sage

Blend all the ingredients well in a food processor or blender and chill. This spread is much tastier if made earlier than required and refrigerated; this allows the flavours to mingle.

Light Tahini

This is a favourite standby. Try the following combinations in these proportions:

> 1 tbsp tahini mixed with ½–1 tsp miso (soya bean paste);
> 1 tbsp tahini mixed with ½ tsp Vecon or Marmite;
> 1 tbsp tahini and 1 or 2 tsp peanut butter (sugar- and salt-free for preference).

SWEET DIPS AND SPREADS

Wedges, slices, and cubes of fruit and sometimes whole, small fruits like strawberries and grapes are ideal for dipping into sweet dips. Always choose predominantly locally grown, seasonal produce but don't forget the more exotic fruits like bananas, pineapples, papayas and mangoes.

The Americans are renowned for their "peanut butter and jelly" sandwiches. We too enjoy nut butters with sweet spreads. How about peanut butter and mashed banana in sandwiches or hot crumpets with peanut butter and apple sauce?

Orange Dream

Preparation time 5 mins.　　　　　*(fills 1 × 12 oz/340g jar)*

8 oz (225g, 1 cup) soft tofu or creamy goats' cheese
2 tbsp frozen orange juice concentrate
2 drops pure orange oil
5 or 6 cardamoms, freshly ground

Blend all the ingredients together in a blender or processor and refrigerate in a screw-top jar. Use the same day.

Carob – Nut Dip

Preparation time 5 mins.　　　　　*(fills 1 × 12 oz/340g jar)*

2 large ripe bananas

2 tbsp peanut butter (sugar- and salt-free if possible)
½–1 tbsp carob powder

Combine all the ingredients together either in a processor or blender or mash with a fork. Mix well. Keeps well in a fridge for 2–3 days.

Carob and Orange Dip
Preparation time 5 mins.   *(fills 1 × 12 oz/340g jar)*

8 oz (225g, 1 cup) soft tofu, mashed firm tofu or quark
2 tbsp frozen orange juice concentrate
1 banana
2 tbsp carob powder
1 tbsp hazelnuts (chopped)
1 orange, cut into small pieces

Blend the tofu or quark, concentrated orange juice, banana and carob powder together to make a fluffy cream. Fold in the hazelnuts and fresh orange. Keeps up to 2 days in the fridge.

Banana and Avocado Dip
Preparation time 5 mins.   *(½ × 12 oz/340g jar)*

½ avocado
1 ripe banana
1 tsp lemon juice

Remove the stone from the avocado. Scoop out its flesh and blend with the banana and lemon juice, using a food processor, liquidiser or blender.

Pineapple Cream Dip
Preparation time 5 mins.   *(½ × 12 oz/340g jar)*

1 tbsp crushed fresh pineapple
1 tbsp freshly grated or dried coconut (sugar-free)
5 fl oz (140ml, ½ cup) goat yoghurt

Stir the pineapple and coconut into the yoghurt and serve.
Use the same day.

Soft Fruit Fluff

Preparation time 5 mins.   *(½ × 12 oz/340g jar)*

4 oz (110g, ½ cup) soft fruit
2 oz (55g, ¼ cup) soft tofu, cream cheese (quark) or
   yoghurt
1 beaten egg white (optional)

Blend the fruit and tofu (or cheese or yoghurt) together and
fold in the beaten egg white. Use the same day.

Fruit Butter

Preparation time 15 mins.   *(½ × 12 oz/340g jar)*
2 tbsp stoned dates
2 tbsp apricots (unsulphured)
2 tsp candied peel (p. 182)

Wash and drain the dates and apricots, put in a pan and
cover with water. Cook until soft and thick. Remove from
the heat, process to a spreading consistency and add the
candied peel. Will keep, refrigerated, for a week.

Sweet Tahini Spreads

..... 1 tbsp tahini and 1 tsp apple juice concentrate diluted
     in 1 tbsp water.
..... 1 tbsp tahini, 1 tbsp goat yoghurt, fruit juice concentrate
     to taste.
..... 1 tbsp tahini, 1 or 2 tsp frozen, grapefruit concentrate
     and 1 tsp raw honey.

COOKED SNACK BASES AND TOPPINGS

This group of more substantial snacks and fillings can be easily mixed and matched with almost any of the dips and spreads in the earlier part of this chapter. Do experiment with alternatives.

Savoury Squares
Preparation time 45 mins.   *(makes 4–6 squares)*

Base
   4 oz (110g, ¾ cup) wholewheat flour (organic)
   3 oz (85g, ¾ cup) oats
   ½ tsp kelp
   3 fl oz (85ml, ⅓ cup) cold-pressed sunflower oil
   2 tbsp tomato purée

Mix all the dry ingredients together. Stir in the oil and the tomato purée to form a soft dough. Press two-thirds of the mixture into a greased 12″ × 8″ (30cm × 20cm) baking pan. Spread a filling (see below) on the dough. Sprinkle the rest of the dough mixture over the top and even it out with a fork. Bake at gas 4 (180°C, 350°F) for about 25 minutes or until cooked and lightly browned. Cut into squares.

For a filling try
   4 oz (110g, 1 cup) mushrooms
   1 small leek
   1 small green pepper
   ghee
   **4 oz (110g, ½ cup) cream cheese or grated vegetarian
      cheddar**
   1 tsp basil (dried) or 1 tbsp chopped fresh basil

Wash and slice the mushrooms, leek and pepper (p. 33). Lightly sauté them all together in a warmed pan which has been brushed with sufficient ghee to prevent them from sticking. Toss them in a bowl with the cheese and basil, and stir well before spreading evenly over the base.

10 Minute Pizza
Preparation time 10 mins.   *(makes 4 small pizzas)*

Base
   6 oz (170g, 1 cup) wholewheat flour (organic)
   1 heaped tsp baking powder (p. 146)
   water to mix
   olive oil for brushing pan and pizza

Mix the flour and baking powder with some water and knead to form a soft dough. Roll out thinly and using a saucer, cut into small rounds. Grease one or two heavy pans by brushing with a little olive oil, heat gently and put in the pizza rounds. Cook for 3 minutes. Turn over and brush the surface of the pizzas with a little more olive oil. Lower the heat and keep the pizza bases in the pan while you add the topping.

Top each with

   1 tsp tomato purée
   ½ tsp basil
   ½ spring onion, chopped
   ½ tomato, sliced
   2 mushrooms, sliced
   **1 tbsp grated (vegetarian) cheddar cheese or grated
       firm tofu, mixed with a pinch of nutmeg or cayenne
       pepper**

Finally, transfer the pizzas to a grill and cook for a few minutes until the cheese or tofu melts.

Yeast-Base Pizzas
                    (makes 3–4 trays, 12" × 8" or 30cm × 20cm)
Preparation time 1 hour

Base

   1 oz (25g) fresh yeast
   1 pt (550ml, 2½ cups) tepid water
   2 lb (900g, 6 cups) wholewheat flour

Topping

   5 fl oz (140ml, ⅔ cup) olive oil
   8 oz (225g, 1 cup) onions
   5 sticks of celery
   1 bunch spring onions
   1 large green pepper
   12 oz (340g, 3 cups) mushrooms
   6 oz (170g, ½ cup) tomato paste
   2 tbsp dried basil or 4 tbsp chopped fresh basil
   12 oz (340g, 3 cups) grated vegetarian cheddar cheese,
      or
   1 pt (550ml, 2 cups) natural yoghurt mixed with 2 eggs

In a bowl, dissolve the yeast in all the water and add
sufficient flour to make a cream. Whisk well. Cover with a
clear polythene bag (p. 34) or a damp tea-towel and leave in a
warm position to prove. This should take about half an
hour. When the yeast begins to bubble, add the remaining
flour, cup by cup, until a "springy" dough is reached. Knead
for 5 minutes if you are making it by hand, 1–2 minutes in a
processor. Grease 3 or 4 pizza trays with a little olive oil. Set
the oven at gas 6 (200°C, 400°F). Break the dough into 3 or 4
equal pieces. Spread one piece thinly over each tray, using
the backs of your fingers to stretch the dough. Leave it to rise
a little while you wash and prepare the vegetables. Chop the
onions, celery and spring onions. Slice the pepper and
mushrooms. Brush the surface of the dough bases with olive
oil, spread the tomato paste evenly over them and sprinkle
on the basil. Top the pizza bases with the vegetables and
finally the grated cheese or yoghurt and egg mixture. Bake in
the hot oven for 25 minutes or until golden brown. Eat the
same day or cool thoroughly and wrap well in greaseproof
paper before covering in freezer film.

   Be adventurous with your toppings – they may not be the
authentic Italian pizza toppings but they make tasty,
economical meals! Alternative combinations could include:
green and red peppers; tomato, garlic and courgettes; celery,
mushrooms and black olives; aubergines dipped in egg with
tomatoes and walnuts etc.

   Another alternative to cheese topping is mock sour cream.
Make by blending 8 oz (225g) firm tofu with 1 tbsp cold-

pressed oil and 2–3 tbsp lemon juice. This can be flavoured too, with the addition of 1 tsp fresh, chopped parsley, 1 finely chopped spring onion and ½ clove of garlic, crushed.

Potato Scones
Preparation time about 1 hour   *(makes 6–8)*

   8 oz (225g) potatoes
   4 oz (110g, ¾ cup) wholewheat flour
   2 tbsp chopped parsley
   1 oz (25g) ghee
   a pinch or two of mustard powder
   ghee for frying

Wash the potatoes thoroughly. Slice them thinly and steam for about 10 minutes until soft. Transfer them to a mixing bowl, mash them and then knead in the remaining ingredients until you have an evenly mixed dough. Press the dough into a ball, leave in the bowl (covered) in the fridge for about an hour. Roll the dough on a floured board and cut into rounds or wedges. Heat a heavy pan, brush it lightly with a little ghee and cook the scones until golden-coloured, turning each one to brown both sides. Will freeze or keep for 2 days in a covered container in the fridge.

Oat Muffins
Preparation time 30 mins.   *(makes 18 small muffins)*

   ghee for greasing trays
   8 oz (225g, 1½ cups) medium oatmeal (organic)
   8 oz (225g, 1⅓ cups) organic wholewheat flour
   1 tsp baking powder (p. 146)
   10 fl oz (300ml, 1¼ cups) vegetable stock (p. 93)
   2 beaten egg whites

Preheat the oven at gas 5 (190°C, 375°F). Grease muffin or small cake trays with a little ghee. Mix the oatmeal, flour and baking powder with the vegetable stock. Beat the egg whites and fold them into the mixture. Spoon into the muffin trays and bake for 20 minutes. Eat immediately or cool thoroughly on a wire tray and freeze.

6

BREAD AND PASTRY

Home-made bread is delicious. Wheat is usually the main grain used in bread-making because it contains plenty of gluten – the proteins in the flour which, with the yeast, produce a light well-risen loaf. However, for variety, we often substitute for a little of the wheat flour in our basic recipe other flours free from or low in gluten like gram flour (chick pea) and maizemeal.

Home-made bread does not have any preservatives in it and so will not keep fresh for more than a day. It does, however, make excellent toast for two further days. Batch baking and freezing bread is useful, preferably sliced to avoid panics on those mornings when none has been defrosted!

We usually use fresh yeast, but sour dough is a good alternative. It is simple to make and produces a heavier loaf.

You may like to brush the tops of your savoury rolls or loaves with beaten egg and sprinkle poppy, caraway or sesame seeds on them before baking. Sweeter breads are attractive if brushed with beaten egg and 2 tsp warmed malt.

Our Quick and Easy Wholewheat Bread
Fills two 2 lb (900g) loaf tins

This can be made in about an hour if your kitchen is warm. I admit to using my processor for the first few stages now, and usually prepare the dough while making a main meal as the oven is hot and the air in the kitchen is not only warm but moist. Once the meal is dished-up the loaves are put in the oven.

1 oz (25g) fresh yeast
1 pt (550ml, 2½ cups) tepid water
2 lb (900g, 6 cups) wholewheat flour (organic)

Dissolve the yeast in all of the water, either in a bowl or food processor bowl. Whisk this mixture for 2 minutes by hand or whizz well in your food processor. Add 2 or 3 cups of flour, enough to make a cream. Place this mixture – still in the bowl – inside a clear polythene bag (p. 34), seal and leave to prove in a warm position. The mixture will bubble and appear spongy when proved. This stage should be reached in about 15 minutes. Too little heat at this stage will simply prolong the operation, but too much heat will kill the yeast and your bread will fail. I stand my bowl on a cooling rack on the heating boiler in the kitchen.

When the mixture has proved, stir with a wooden spoon or whizz it for a few seconds in the processor. Add the remaining flour one cupful at a time and knead between each addition of flour. Remember that each batch of wholewheat flour behaves differently and that you may not need to use all of the flour or you may need more depending on how absorbent it is.

Preheat the oven at gas 6 (200°C, 400°F). Knead the dough well for about 10 minutes – it should become light and springy to the touch. (I find that if I have added most of the flour in the processor and mixed it well I do not have to knead for more than a minute or two as I work in the remaining flour by hand.)

Grease two 2 lb loaf tins (or one × 4 lb), put the dough in them and press it down with your knuckles to half fill them. Place the tins in the polythene bag and leave the dough to prove as before. It should double in size. When the dough reaches the top of the tins put the bread into the preheated oven and bake for 35 minutes. Take the loaves out of the tins and return them to the oven, upside down, for 10 minutes at gas 4 or "off" in an electric oven. Test the loaves by tapping on the bottom – if they sound hollow they are cooked. If not, return them to the oven for a further 5 minutes. Cool on a cooling rack. If you wish to have a soft crust, cover your loaves with a clean tea-towel whilst they cool. Consume within 2 days or freeze, sliced.

Pitta Pockets: using the same recipe, break off 6 small balls of dough and allow these to double in size. Roll them out into oval shapes on a floured board and then bake on greased baking trays in a hot oven gas 7 (220°C, 425°F) for about 10 minutes.

VARIATIONS ON THE BASIC BREAD

Rye Bread: replace half of the wheat flour with rye flour which is low in gluten or a quarter rye and a quarter fine oatmeal. Also try using half buttermilk and half water as the liquid.

Herby Rolls: include 1 tbsp Tamari soy sauce in the water and add 2 tsp dried sage, 2 tsp chopped dried chives and 1 tsp linseeds to the flour. If you have fresh herbs, use 2 tbsp of each. Break up the dough and form balls of about 2″ (5cm) in diameter. Press your thumb into the centre of the underside and tuck the edges under to prevent the rolls from spreading. Place them on a greased baking sheet and cook at gas 6 (200°C, 400°F) for 20 minutes.

To prevent a hard crust forming, cover the rolls with a clean cloth whilst they are cooling on a wire rack.

Seed Bread: add 2 tbsp chopped pan-roasted sunflower seeds or other – sesame, poppy, caraway (not necessarily roasted). Sprouted seeds are also delicious in bread – add 2 handfuls to the flour at the beginning.

Malty Fruit Bread: add 8 oz (225g, 1⅓ cups) sultanas (unsulphured and free of mineral oils etc.) and 2 tsp cinnamon to the flour, and add 2 tbsp of malt extract and 1 tbsp blackstrap molasses to the yeast and water mixture. Try using granary flour instead of wholewheat flour for a change. Bake at gas 5 (190°C, 375°F) for about 1 hour.

Banana Bread: add 3 small, very ripe, mashed bananas to

14 fl oz (400ml, 1¾ cups) warm soya, goats' or cows' milk instead of water and add 2 tbsp malt or date purée to the yeast before working in the flour.

Buckwheat Loaf

Fills two 1 lb (450g) loaf tins

Preparation time 1½–2 hours

12 oz (340g, 2½ cups) buckwheat flour
12 oz (340g, 3 cups) brown rice flour
8 oz (220g, 3 cups) soya flour
1 oz (25g) fresh yeast
1 pt (550ml, 2½ cups) tepid water or vegetable stock
  (this could be the water from vegetables cooking or
  water with 1 tsp Vecon etc. – see p. 23 added to it)
1 tbsp blackstrap molasses
3 tbsp cold-pressed sesame or corn oil
ghee

Combine the flours in a large mixing bowl. Dissolve the yeast in the water or stock with the molasses added to it. Stir in sufficient of the combined flours to make a creamy consistency. Fork the oil into the remaining flour and then slowly combine both mixtures. Place the resulting dough in a bowl inside a clear polythene bag and leave in a warm place to rise. The top of a heating boiler is ideal; too high a temperature will kill the yeast. Take the dough out of the bag when it has almost doubled in size. Knead gently for 2 or 3 minutes, then divide it equally into two 1 lb (450g) loaf tins greased with ghee. The mixture should half fill each one. Heat the oven to gas 6 (200°C, 400°F). Place the loaves in the tins back inside the clear polythene bag and leave to rise again until doubled in size whilst the oven warms up. Bake for 30–35 minutes and then for a further 10 minutes out of the tins at gas 4 or "off" if using an electric cooker. Cool on wire trays and consume within 2 days or freeze.

Indian Flat-Breads

You need very little fat in this recipe.

Preparation time 40 mins.   *(makes 6–8 approx.)*

1 lb (450g, 3 cups) wholewheat flour (organic)
8 fl oz (225ml, 1 cup) water, approx.
ghee

Put the flour in a bowl and slowly mix in the water, to form a stiff dough. Cover the bowl and leave the dough to stand in a warm place for half an hour at least. Break off small pieces and roll into balls. Roll each ball out on a floured board into an oval shape, 2½″ (6cm) wide and ¼″ (5mm) thick. Heat an *ungreased* heavy pan. Place one or more breads in the pan depending on its size and cook for 2 minutes. Turn and cook the other side. Lightly brush each bread with a little ghee and return to the pan to brown, one side at a time. Serve hot, to complement a full Indian meal, or serve cold, in a packed lunch with a bowl of curry dip and a cucumber and yoghurt salad. Eat the same day.

Stuffed Indian Breads

Savoury and sweet variations on the above recipe are simple.

After the bread has been rolled out, spread a little cooked mashed potato, other vegetables or fruits, herbs or spices on to the middle of it, bring the edges into the centre and roll it out again. Once again do not grease the pan. Continue as for the preceding recipe above.

Breadsticks

Preparation time 20 mins.

Roll out any left-over bread dough into the shape of a rectangle, ¼″ (5mm) thick. Cut strips ½″ (1½cm) wide and roll each strip into a long cylindrical stick. Place on a baking tray, lightly greased with ghee. Bake in a hot oven gas 6 (200°C, 400°F) for 10–15 minutes while baking your bread or pizzas. Store in an airtight container and consume within 2 days.

PASTRY

Unlike bread dough, pastry is most successful when conditions are cold or very cool. Use a metal spoon or blade and do not handle the mixture except to bind it together.

Remember the importance of the correct and safe usage of oils mentioned in Chapter 3. If you find sesame oil too expensive then use it only occasionally. Use butter instead and simply eat pastry less frequently.

Vary your choice of grains. We particularly enjoy pastry made with equal quantities of organic wholewheat flour and fine or medium organic oatmeal or organic wholewheat and organic millet meal made by grinding millet grain in a food grinder. We often substitute 2 oz (55g) of the flour with 2 oz (55g) of wheatgerm or ground sunflower seeds. Sometimes we make the pastry with 3 oz (85g) millet meal, 3 oz (85g) wholewheat flour and 2 oz (55g) maizemeal.

Pastry can be frozen successfully.

Basic Pastry Recipe (made with oil)
(makes 1 × 10" (25cm) flan case)
Preparation time about 45 mins.

8 oz (225g, 1⅓ cups) wholewheat flour (organic)
3 fl oz (85ml, ⅓ cup) cold-pressed sesame oil
4–6 tbsp iced water combined with 1 tsp fresh lemon juice

Using a metal knife or fork, combine the flour and oil. Slowly add the water with lemon juice. We normally add the full amount or even a little more. Wholewheat flour varies in absorbency from one batch to the next. The mixture should be slightly wet at this stage. Place your mixing bowl and pastry in a polythene bag and refrigerate it for at least half an hour while the flour absorbs the water fully. Roll out your pastry on a floured board. Bake as required.

Rich Wholewheat Pastry (made with butter)

(makes 1 × 10" (25cm) flan case)
Preparation time about 45 mins.

   8 oz (225g, 1⅓ cups) wholewheat flour (organic)
   4 oz (110g, ½ cup) butter (at room temperature)
   4 tbsp (approx.) iced water mixed with 1 tsp lemon juice

Put the flour and butter in a bowl. Break the butter into pieces and coat them with the flour. Then rub them into the flour between your fingertips, raising your hands high as much as possible to keep the mixture cool and to incorporate plenty of air. Continue until the mixture resembles fine breadcrumbs. Add the water and lemon juice slowly, mixing it in with a knife, until the mixture binds together. Draw the mixture into a ball using your hands as lightly and quickly as possible. Leave the pastry dough in its bowl and cover it with a polythene bag. Place it in the fridge for at least half an hour. Roll out the uncooked pastry dough on a floured board remembering to keep it cool. Bake as required.

Pastry Crispbreads
Preparation time 15 mins.

Roll out left-over pastry mixture as thinly as possible into long rectangles. Sprinkle the entire surface lightly with dried sage and chives. Fold the bottom third over the centre third and the top third over the first two folded thirds. Roll out the dough again to ¼" (½cm) thickness and cut into rectangles. Place on a baking tray greased with ghee and bake in a hot oven (gas 5, 190°C, 375°F) for about 10 minutes or until cooked and golden in colour. Cool on a wire tray. Store in an airtight container and consume within 2 days. These make an ideal savoury snack on their own or with dips.

7

SALADS AND
SALAD DRESSINGS

Salads are a substantial part of each of our meals. We have
fresh and dried fruit salads at breakfast, and green or more
colourful vegetable salads at lunch and at dinner. Sometimes
tossed in a delicious dressing they accompany a main meal;
sometimes suitably cut raw fruits and vegetables make dip-
sticks for a starter or a snack; sometimes a glorious salad is
itself the main dish.

To complement a main dish, more than one salad, each
made from one or two ingredients, is more interesting than
one large mixed salad. Occasionally combine raw with
cooked, vegetables with fruit or, for a more substantial
salad, cooked chilled pasta, rice or other grain with fresh raw
saladings. Don't forget your home-grown bean, seed and
grain sprouts. They make inexpensive and most nutritious
salads.

GENERAL SALAD HINTS

Always prepare your salad just before serving for the

maximum nutritional value unless the recipe states otherwise. Fresh raw vegetables lose many vitamins when exposed to air, heat and light.

Wash all salad ingredients thoroughly. See p. 33.

Dry well either in a clean tea-towel, a salad basket or a spinner before adding a dressing.

In most of our salad ideas, we have included a favourite dressing. However in the second half of this chapter you will find plenty of alternative dressings to try.

Once dressed, a salad will not stay crisp and fresh.

SALAD RECIPES

Tangy Avocado Salad
Preparation time 5–10 mins.   *(serves 4–6)*

1 large cucumber
2 grapefruits
2 large ripe avocados
1 clove of garlic, crushed
1 tbsp cider vinegar or lemon juice
fresh mint to garnish

Wash the cucumber. Slice it thinly and put in a salad bowl. Peel the grapefruits and chop the segments into small pieces. Add to the cucumber. For the dressing, purée the avocado flesh and combine it with the garlic, and cider vinegar or lemon juice. Spoon onto the salad and toss well. Eat immediately as the avocado discolours after a while even with the addition of lemon juice.

White Cabbage and Caraway Salad
Preparation time 5–10 mins.   *(serves 4–6)*

½ small white cabbage
½–1 tsp caraway seeds
¼ tsp mustard powder
2 tsp cider vinegar
4 tsp cold-pressed sunflower oil

Wash the cabbage (p. 33) and remove any tough outer leaves (these can go into a stock-pot if organic). Shred it and put into a salad bowl with the caraway seeds. Make the dressing by combining the mustard, cider vinegar and oil, and mixing well. Pour over the cabbage and caraway salad and toss before serving.

White Cabbage and Apricot Salad
Preparation time 5–10 mins.   *(serves 4–6 people)*

½ **small white cabbage**
10 dried apricots (unsulphured)
juice of 2 large grapefruits
4 tsp cold-pressed grapeseed oil

Wash the cabbage (p. 33) and shred it finely. Wash and chop the apricots. Combine in a salad bowl. Mix the fruit juice and oil together, pour onto the salad and toss well, before serving.

Salad of Calabrese, Avocado and Grapefruit
Preparation time 5–10 mins.   *(serves 4–6)*

8 oz (225g) calabrese
1 avocado
1 grapefruit
grapefruit juice

Wash the calabrese (p. 33), peel the avocado and grapefruit. Slice the avocado and discard the stone. Arrange the florets of calabrese, slices of avocado and segments of grapefruit in the bottom of your salad bowl and toss with a little grapefuit juice. Serve immediately.

Watercress Salad
Preparation time 5–10 mins.   *(serves 4–6)*

1 bunch watercress or American land cress

orange or grapefruit segments
4 oz (110g, ½ cup) hazelnuts, chopped
4 oz (110g, ½ cup) corn kernels, fresh or frozen
juice of 1 orange or grapefruit
seasoning – sprinkling of spirulina or other of choice

Wash the cress thoroughly (p. 33). Arrange it decoratively in a serving bowl with the orange or grapefruit segments, hazelnuts and corn kernels. Add the orange or grapefruit juice and finally a sprinkling of spirulina.

Pear and Grape Salad
Preparation time 10 mins.   *(serves 4)*

1 lettuce
2 fresh pears
4 oz (110g) fresh black grapes
1 tsp chives, chopped
2 tbsp home-made cottage cheese, quark or mashed,
    firm tofu

Wash the lettuce, pears, grapes and chives (p. 33). Cut the pears in half, remove the cores and carefully spoon out most of the flesh. Chop this and add to the cheese or mashed tofu and add the chopped chives. Arrange the lettuce on a serving plate, fill the pears with the cheese or tofu mixture, top with the black grapes (stoned), place on the bed of lettuce leaves and serve.

Carrot and Sugar Pea Salad
Preparation time 1 hour 10 mins.   *(serves 6)*

4 large carrots
2 oz (55g) sugar peas or mangetout
4 tbsp virgin olive oil
4 tbsp brown rice vinegar
2 tsp Tamari soy sauce
1–2 tsp grated fresh root ginger

Wash the carrots and sugar peas, peeling the carrots if not organic (p. 33). Steam the sugar peas lightly for 3 minutes, remove from the steamer and cool by laying them out on a sheet of paper towel. Make the dressing by combining the oil, brown rice vinegar, Tamari soy sauce and grated ginger. Grate the carrots, place them in a salad bowl with the sugar peas and stir in the dressing. Cover and leave in a cool place for at least an hour to allow the flavours to merge.

Sweet Carrot Salad
Preparation time 10 mins.   *(serves 6)*

4 large carrots
1 handful raisins (black for colour contrast)
1 tbsp lemon juice
1 tsp malt
1 tsp molasses

Wash the carrots and raisins thoroughly (p. 33). Grate the carrots and put them in a salad bowl with the raisins. Make the dressing by combining the lemon juice, malt and molasses together (use a heated spoon to measure the malt and molasses as this will thin them slightly and facilitate mixing). Add to the carrot salad, toss well and serve immediately.

Green Spinach and Red Onion Salad
Preparation time 10 mins.   *(serves 4–6)*

4 fresh spinach leaves
2 medium red onions
½ clove of garlic
2 tbsp cold-pressed virgin olive oil
2 tsp wine or cider vinegar
½–1 tsp raw honey (optional)
½ tsp mustard

Wash and prepare the spinach and onions (p. 33), spinning the spinach dry before chopping it. Slice the onions. Rub the inside of a salad bowl with the open edge of half of the clove of garlic and then put in the chopped spinach and sliced onions. Make the dressing by crushing the garlic and combining it with all the remaining ingredients and mixing well. Pour over the salad and toss thoroughly just before serving.

Spicy Beetroot Salad

Preparation time 1 hour 10 mins.   *(serves 4–6)*

  4 small young beetroot
  1 handful sultanas (unsulphured)
  1 tbsp cider vinegar
  2 tbsp fresh orange juice
  1–2 tsp raw honey
  1 heaped tsp freshly grated ginger
  grated rind of organic or unsprayed orange

Wash, peel and grate the beetroot as finely as possible. Wash and cloth-dry the sultanas and put them into a salad bowl with the grated beetroot. Combine the cider vinegar, orange juice, honey and ginger together and mix well. Pour over the beetroot salad, and toss vigorously. Decorate with the grated orange rind, cover, and refrigerate for at least an hour before serving.

White Cabbage Salad with a Mediterranean Flavour

Preparation time 10 mins.   *(serves 6)*

  ½ small white cabbage, shredded
  5 large spring onions
  12 oz (340g, 1½ cups) tomatoes
  2 tbsp virgin olive oil
  1 tbsp cider or wine vinegar
  1 tsp malt
  2 tbsp chopped fresh sweet basil or 2 tsp dried basil
  1 clove of garlic, crushed

Wash and prepare the cabbage and onions (p. 33) putting all tough outside skins (if organic) aside for the stock-pot. Shred the cabbage coarsely and chop the onions. Arrange them in a salad bowl. Wash the tomatoes and mash them into a purée – peeling is only necessary if the tomatoes are very large and tough-skinned. Combine the oil, vinegar, malt, basil and crushed garlic and add to the mashed tomatoes. Pour this tomato dressing over the shredded cabbage and onion salad and toss well, before serving.

Gingered White Cabbage
Preparation time 10 mins.   *(serves 6)*

  ½ small white cabbage
  2 large carrots
  5 spring onions
  4 fl oz (110ml, ½ cup) fresh orange or pineapple juice
  3 tbsp tahini
  juice of 1 lemon
  1 tsp Tamari soy sauce
  1 tsp freshly grated ginger

Wash and prepare the cabbage, carrots and spring onions (p. 33), putting all outside tough leaves of the cabbage aside for the stock-pot if organic. Shred the cabbage, grate the carrots and chop the onions and place them in a salad bowl. Blend all the remaining ingredients together in a liquidiser or processor or beat vigorously with a hand whisk. Add this dressing to the salad and toss well.

White Cabbage with Cashew Mayonnaise
Preparation time 10 mins.   *(serves 6)*

  ½ small white cabbage
  2 carrots
  1 small onion
  2 tbsp raisins

2 tbsp raw cashews
½ clove of garlic, crushed
2 tbsp water
2 tbsp cold-pressed sunflower or grapeseed oil
1 tbsp lemon juice

Wash the cabbage, carrots, onion and raisins (p. 33). Keep the tough outside leaves of the cabbage, if organic, for the stock-pot. Shred the cabbage, grate the carrots and chop the onion and put all these vegetables together with the raisins into a salad bowl. Process or grind the cashews finely and then, using a liquidiser, blender or food processor, blend with the garlic and water. Add the oil, trickling it in very slowly, and beating or blending all the time until the mixture thickens. Add the lemon juice. Spoon this mayonnaise onto the salad and mix well. Will keep up to a day, covered and refrigerated.

Soy Slaw
Preparation time 10 mins.   *(serves 6)*

½ small white cabbage
2 large carrots
1 tbsp chopped dates
2 tbsp silken tofu (you can blend 1 tbsp firm tofu with
   1 tbsp water if silken is not available)
1 tbsp tahini
1 tsp lemon juice
2 tbsp water

Wash and shred the cabbage, wash and grate the carrots as in the previous recipe and put them in a salad bowl with the chopped dates. Using a liquidiser, blender or food processor blend all the other ingredients together, adding more water if the mayonnaise becomes too thick. Pour over the salad and mix well. This slaw will keep up to one day in an airtight container in the fridge.

Leek and Tomato Vinaigrette
Preparation time 1 hour 20 mins.   *(serves 4)*

4 slim young leeks
4 tsp wine vinegar
1–2 cloves of garlic, crushed
seasoning – spirulina and freshly ground black pepper
4 tbsp virgin olive oil
8 medium-ripe but firm salad tomatoes

Wash and trim the leeks, putting aside any tough outside
leaves for the stock-pot if organic. Cut them in half
lengthwise and steam for 5–10 minutes or until cooked.
Remove from the pan and leave to cool either in the steamer
or in a colander while you prepare the tomatoes and
dressing. Combine the vinegar, garlic and seasoning and
slowly add the oil. Arrange the leeks on a flat serving dish.
Wash the tomatoes and slice them thinly. Intersperse these
slices among the leeks. Pour the dressing over the salad,
cover well to prevent the salad's strong aroma from
overwhelming everything else in your fridge and chill for at
least an hour.

Classic French Tomato Vinaigrette
Preparation time 10 mins.   *(serves 4)*

8 large, ripe, firm tomatoes
1 large onion
1–2 cloves of garlic, crushed
seasoning – sea salt or kelp, freshly ground black pepper
4 tsp cider vinegar
4 tbsp cold-pressed sunflower oil
2 tbsp chopped fresh herbs – parsley, chervil and/or
    tarragon

Wash (p. 33) and then thinly slice the tomatoes. Peel and
slice the onion. Break up the onion slices into rings. Rub the
cut edge of a clove of garlic over the surface of your salad
bowl. Arrange the tomato slices and onion rings in it and
sprinkle seasoning of your choice over them. Make the

vinaigrette dressing by mixing the vinegar and garlic
together and then slowly blending in the oil. Beat well. Pour
the dressing over the salad and top it with the chopped
parsley – the more the better as parsley is not only highly
nutritious but it also lessens the powerful scent of the garlic
on your breath.

Try chopped chives instead of onion for variety or add 2
hard-boiled eggs, sliced or cut into wedges.

Potato, Apple and Avocado Salad
Preparation time 15 mins.   *(serves 3–4)*

1 large potato
1 avocado
1 large eating apple
1 crisp lettuce
juice of 2 lemons
2 tbsp virgin olive oil
black pepper

Wash and slice the potato (p. 33) and steam the slices for
5–10 minutes until cooked but firm. Allow to cool. Peel the
avocado, and wash or peel the apple. Wash the lettuce and
break it into small pieces, dice the apple and slice the
avocado flesh, discarding the stone. Squeeze the lemon juice
over the apple and avocado at once to stem discoloration.
Arrange the cooked potato on top of the lettuce pieces on a
serving platter. Drizzle the olive oil all over both and
sprinkle with seasoning. Now scatter the apple and avocado
pieces evenly over the whole platter. Serve immediately.

New Potato Salad
Preparation time 15-20 mins.   *(serves 6)*

1½ lb (675g) small new potatoes
4 tbsp virgin olive oil
4 tsp wine or cider vinegar
½ tsp mustard
4 cold hard-boiled eggs
1 tbsp chopped herbs – parsley and tarragon

Wash the new potatoes (p. 33) and steam them lightly for about 10 minutes. Allow them to cool. Place them on a serving platter and dress them with a vinaigrette dressing made from the olive oil, vinegar and mustard. Sprinkle with the chopped eggs and herbs.

Green Beans and Almonds
Preparation time 45 mins.   *(serves 4)*

    8 oz (225g) green beans
    1 oz (25g, ¼ cup) almonds
    2 tbsp cold-pressed sesame oil
    1 tbsp lemon juice
    ½–1 clove of garlic, crushed
    1 tbsp finely chopped fresh chervil or parsley

Wash and steam the beans lightly for 5–10 minutes. Let them cool and then place them in a salad bowl with the almonds. Mix the oil, lemon juice and garlic together well and pour over both the beans and almonds.

Sprinkle with chopped fresh chervil, cover and chill before serving. Try this salad without the oil in the dressing for a refreshing change.

Red Bean Salad
Preparation time 10 mins.   *(serves 4–6)*

    1 clove of garlic
    ½ tsp mustard powder
    4 tsp wine or cider vinegar
    4 tbsp virgin olive oil
    1 lb (450g, 2 cups) cooked red kidney beans (p. 33)
    4 tomatoes
    1 large onion
    2 tbsp chopped herbs – tarragon and parsley

Rub around the inside of a salad bowl with the cut edge of the clove of garlic and then crush it to add to the dressing. (Make the dressing by vigorously combining the mustard, crushed garlic, vinegar and oil.) Put the beans in the bowl. Wash the tomatoes (p. 33) and peel the onion. Slice both. Break the onion slices into rings. Arrange the tomatoes and onion rings on top of the beans and pour the dressing over all the ingredients. Sprinkle with the herbs and serve.

Green Bean and Olive Salad
Preparation time 25 mins.   *(serves 6)*

4 eggs
8 oz (225 g) green beans
1 lb (450g) tomatoes
2 medium onions
12 pitted black olives
1 clove of garlic, crushed
2 tbsp lemon juice
4 tbsp virgin olive oil
2 tbsp chopped herbs – parsley, tarragon and chives

Boil the eggs for 10 minutes until hard-boiled and then cool them in their shells under cold running water. Wash (p. 33), trim and steam the green beans for 5–10 minutes until cooked but still crunchy. While they cool, wash and slice the tomatoes. Peel the onions, slice and break them into rings. Shell the eggs and cut them into wedges. Arrange the beans, tomatoes and onion rings decoratively in a serving dish and top with the black olives and wedges of the hard-boiled eggs. Combine the crushed garlic, lemon juice and olive oil, mix well and pour over the salad. Top with chopped herbs and serve.

* Any left-over cooked beans (p. 33) – French beans, red kidney beans, white haricots etc. – can be turned successfully into a salad. The variations are endless. If you want a change from the oil and vinegar dressings try some of the creamy ones which follow on page 90.

Chick Pea Salad
Preparation time 20 mins.   *(serves 6–8)*

> **8 oz (225g, 1½ cups) cooked chick peas**
> **1 lb (450g) mixed fresh vegetables – peas, French beans, carrots, young leeks, peppers, celery, tomatoes**
> **4 fl oz (110ml, ½ cup) egg mayonnaise (p. 87) with garlic**

Wash (p. 33) and prepare the vegetables, cutting, dicing or chopping as desired – the smaller the pieces the better. Steam lightly for 5 minutes. When cool, place all the ingredients in a bowl with the salad dressing and toss until all the vegetables are coated with mayonnaise. Will keep for a day or two in an airtight container in the fridge.

Tabbouleh
                             (serves 4–6)
Preparation time 10 mins., overnight in fridge
   and then 40 mins.

> **8 oz (225g, 1⅓ cups) bulgar wheat**
> **12 fl oz (350ml, 1½ cups) boiling water**
> **2 handfuls mint**
> **1 handful parsley**
> **4 tbsp virgin olive oil**
> **4 tbsp lemon juice**
> **1 lb (450g) tomatoes, chopped**
> **1 medium cucumber, diced**

Rinse the bulgar wheat, cover with the boiling water and leave to stand for about 20 minutes or until all the water has been absorbed. Wash (p. 33) and chop the mint and parsley as finely as possible. Combine the oil, lemon juice and herbs and stir into the bulgar wheat. Cover the salad and leave in the fridge overnight. Fold the chopped tomatoes and diced cucumber into the bulgar salad half an hour before serving. Will keep for a day in a covered container in the fridge.

Fruit and Nut Mix
Preparation time 15 mins.   (serves 6)

   4 large carrots
   a good handful of each – sunflower seeds, peanuts,
      raisins
   1 tbsp pumpkin seeds
   juice of 1 lemon
   ½ small pineapple, cubed
   1 tbsp peanut butter (sugar- and salt-free preferably)
   2 tbsp soya yoghurt (or other)

Wash the carrots, seeds and raisins (p. 33). Grate the carrots, sprinkle with the lemon juice and combine with the seeds, raisins and pineapple in a serving bowl. Blend the peanut butter with the yoghurt either with a hand whisk or in a liquidiser or processor. Stir into the salad and mix well. This salad is great in packed lunches served in pitta pockets (p. 67) with an undressed green salad as the main course. It will keep up to 2 days in the fridge.

Green Salads With A Difference
There are many easily cultivated green leafed plants that may not appear in supermarkets. Try mixing many green leaves for an attractive and tasty salad: flat lettuce, crisp Iceberg lettuce, young dandelion leaves, purslane, leek tops, chick-weed, nasturtium leaves, carrot tops, chard, broccoli, chicory and endive all become more enticing when mixtures are interlaced for variety.

SALAD DRESSINGS

Most of the following recipes for dressings do contain oil but many of them are just as delicious without. Fresh fruit juices or crushed sunflower or pumpkin seeds with lemon juice make wonderful dressings and there are lots of simple but imaginative variations on this theme for which I need hardly give individual recipes.

A dressing should enhance a salad and not overwhelm it. The recipes which follow are ones with which we love to experiment on our salads. We hope you will try them on your own salad concoctions, as well as using as variations to our salad recipes in the first half of this chapter.

VINAIGRETTES

French Vinaigrette
Preparation time 5 mins.

  4 tsp wine or cider vinegar
  freshly ground pepper
  pinch of sea salt or kelp
  ½-1 tsp malt or honey (optional)
  4 tbsp olive oil

Mix the vinegar, seasoning and malt or honey before slowly blending in the oil using a fork, liquidiser or food processor. Multiple amounts can be made and stored in a screw-top jar.

Mixed Herb Vinaigrette
Preparation time 3 mins.

  2 tbsp vinaigrette, as in above recipe
  1 tbsp chopped fresh chives
  1 tbsp chopped fresh parsley
  1 tsp chopped fresh marjoram or ½ tsp dried
  1 tsp chopped fresh thyme or ½ tsp dried

Combine all the ingredients together. Use freshly made.

Variations on this Theme
To the above French vinaigrette recipe add:

..... ½ tsp mustard
..... or a forked hard-boiled egg with 2 tsp chopped parsley
       and 2 tsp chopped tarragon, and substitute lemon juice
       for the vinegar

..... or 2 tbsp mashed blue cheese (try Ewe's Blue)
..... or a combination of herbs, e.g. parsley, tarragon and chervil; basil, mint, marjoram, thyme and chives
..... or ½–¾ tsp tangy pepper sauce or tabasco, and 2 tbsp chopped mixed herbs
..... or raw onion, garlic and capers.

MAYONNAISES

Egg Mayonnaise
Preparation time 5 mins.

> 1 egg yolk (free-range, p. 24)
> ½ tsp mustard powder
> 2 tsp lemon juice or cider vinegar
> pinch of kelp and black pepper
> 5 fl oz (150ml, ⅔ cup) cold-pressed oil – sunflower, safflower, olive, or a mixture of half sunflower oil and half olive oil

Combine the egg yolk, mustard, lemon juice or cider vinegar and seasoning, and beat well. Continue to whisk the mixture as you trickle in the oil. The oil must be beaten into the egg yolk quickly for the mayonnaise to thicken but it must be added very slowly, drop by drop whilst the quick beating progresses. One egg yolk can take about double this amount of oil so continue adding if you wish to fill a jar. Mayonnaise will keep in a screw-top jar for about 5 days. Do not refrigerate as the eggs will separate from the oil.

Aioli is a delicious mayonnaise or dip made as in the previous recipe with the addition of 2 crushed cloves of garlic at the end of the procedure.

Yoghurt Mayonnaise
Preparation time 5 mins.

> 1–2 tsp lemon juice
> ½–1 clove of garlic (crushed)

pinch of nutmeg
1 tbsp cold-pressed oil
2 tbsp natural goat or soy yoghurt (p. 37)

Mix the lemon juice, garlic and seasoning together with a
fork or in a blender or food processor. Slowly trickle in the
oil and finally blend all the ingredients with the yoghurt.

MAYONNAISE VARIATIONS

..... Half goat yoghurt, half mayonnaise.

..... Yoghurt, egg mayonnaise, dill weed, parsley and
chives.

..... Add a little curry powder or ground cumin to egg or
yoghurt mayonnaise.

..... 1 tbsp peanut butter or tahini per 3 tbsp egg or yoghurt
mayonnaise, plus 1 tsp lemon juice, pinch of cayenne.

..... 3 tbsp egg or yoghurt mayonnaise mixed with 1 tbsp
creamy goat cheese, 1 tbsp chopped chives, 1 tbsp
chopped parsley, pinch of cayenne.

..... 6 tbsp egg or yoghurt mayonnaise, 1 tbsp tomato juice,
2 tbsp finely chopped vegetables in lactic acid.

..... 1 avocado, 2 tbsp egg or yoghurt mayonnaise, 1 tbsp
lemon juice, seasoning (spirulina, nutritional yeast).

..... 4 tbsp cottage cheese, 1 tbsp egg mayonnaise and
1 tbsp yoghurt plus 1 crushed clove of garlic and 2 tbsp
chopped parsley.

Soyannaise
A thick sauce with soya flour, soya milk and arrowroot.
Preparation time 10 mins.

8 fl oz (225ml, 1 cup) water or soya milk
2 heaped tbsp soya flour
1 heaped tbsp arrowroot
8 tbsp water
1 tbsp lemon juice
½ clove garlic, crushed
4 fl oz (110ml, ½ cup) cold-pressed safflower or
sunflower oil

Warm the milk. Mix the soya flour and arrowroot to a paste with the water and stir that into the warmed milk. Bring to the boil and continue to stir for 3 minutes or until thick. Remove from the heat and cool. Blend in a liquidiser or food processor with lemon juice, garlic and oil. Store in a screw-top jar in the fridge. Will keep for 2 to 3 days but may need blending again before use.

Tofu Mayonnaise
Preparation time 5 mins.

1 lb (450g) firm or soft tofu (p. 185)
½ tsp mustard
¼ tsp kelp
2 tsp barley malt or 1 tsp honey
4 tbsp cold-pressed sunflower oil
4 tbsp cider vinegar

Using a liquidiser, blender or food processor blend all the ingredients together until smooth and creamy.

Try also:

..... tofu mayonnaise mixed with chopped celery, onion and finely chopped pickled vegetables (in natural lactic acid);
..... tofu mayonnaise flavoured with 1 clove of garlic (crushed), ½ tsp dill weed, ½ tsp soy sauce;
..... tofu sour cream – 1 lb (450g) soft or firm tofu curdled with 2 tbsp lemon juice;
..... 8 oz (225g) tofu, 2 tbsp tomato purée, 2 tbsp lemon juice, 1–2 cloves of garlic (crushed), 1 tbsp freshly chopped basil.

Cashew Dressing
Substitute this cashew dressing for any mayonnaise.
Preparation time 5 mins.

1 cup cashews
½ clove of garlic

pinch cayenne pepper
1 cup water
2–3 tbsp cold-pressed sunflower oil
1 tbsp lemon juice

Process the cashews, garlic, seasoning and water until smooth (you will need to soak the nuts overnight if you do not have a food processor). Continue to blend the mixture as you slowly add the oil. Add the lemon juice last when the dressing is thick. Will keep for 2 days in a screw-top jar in the fridge.

* A combination of sunflower seeds and sesame seeds which have been soaked and ground can be used instead of the cashews.

CREAMY DRESSINGS

Here are some "instant" creamy dressings, made in a moment. In each case blend all the given ingredients together to make a smooth cream, adding the liquids last so that you can judge the right amount without drowning the dressing.

..... Use 1 part water to 2 parts tahini, fresh orange juice to taste (the frozen pure concentrate gives more flavour).
..... 1 tbsp tahini, 4 oz (110g) soft tofu, ½– 1 tsp Tamari soy sauce, 1 tbsp lemon juice, 1 clove of garlic (crushed), water to thin the dressing.
..... 1 ripe avocado, concentrated pure grapefruit juice.
..... 2 parts tahini, 1 part water, lemon juice, and Tamari soy sauce to taste.

Yoghurt Herb Dressing
Preparation time 3 mins.

2 tsp lemon juice or cider vinegar
1 tsp malt
1 tsp each of tarragon, basil, marjoram
2 tbsp natural yoghurt

Mix the lemon juice or vinegar, malt and herbs together. Stir in the yoghurt and beat well.

Pesto
Preparation time 5 mins.

   large handful of sweet basil
   2 oz (55g) pine nuts or walnuts
   1–2 cloves of garlic
   1–2 oz (25–55g) feta, or grated vegetarian cheddar cheese
   5 fl oz (150ml, ⅔ cup) olive oil

Chop the sweet basil and walnuts if you are using them instead of pine nuts, crush the garlic and grate the cheese. Combine all the ingredients and beat well. Keeps for 2 days in a screw-top jar in the fridge.

Tomato Caper Dressing
Preparation time 5 mins.

   8 oz (225g, 1 cup) chopped, mashed tomatoes
   juice of 1 lemon
   2 tsp capers
   2 cloves of garlic, crushed
   1 tbsp virgin olive oil

Combine all these ingredients together in a mixing bowl and beat well with a fork. Will keep for 2 days in a screw-top jar in the fridge.

SALAD STARTERS

All our salad recipes make excellent starters to main meals. A few more ideas follow.

Avocado Boats
Preparation time 10 mins.   *(serves 4)*

2 avocados (½ avocado per person)
½ tsp frozen fresh grapefruit juice concentrate
1 tsp frozen fresh orange juice concentrate
juice of ½ lemon
1 grapefruit
garnish – thin slices of orange and sprigs of fresh mint

Cut the avocados in half, remove and discard the stones, and
spoon out the flesh and mix it with the juice concentrates and
lemon juice. Peel the grapefruit, break into segments and
chop each into small pieces. Add to the avocado mixture.
Pile back into the avocado skins and serve garnished with
thin orange slices and sprigs of mint.

Grilled Grapefruit
Preparation time 3 mins.

½ grapefruit per person
malt
orange segments for garnish

Simply cut around the inner edge of the grapefruit and
between the segments. Using a heated spoon add ½–1 tsp
malt on the top of each grapefruit half. Grill until bubbling
and lightly brown. Garnish and serve immediately.

8

SOUPS

Home-made soups are easy to make, inexpensive and far more nutritious than those out of tins or packets. There are delicious raw soups and then there are cooked soups. The latter may be served chilled or piping hot according to type and taste.

There are certain essential ingredients in good tasty soups.

STOCK

Stock is the liquid base for most of the soups we concoct. It retains important minerals and creates flavour. We reckon on a minimum of 2 pints (1100ml, 5 cups) of stock going into a soup for 4 servings. It is easy to make.

1. Keep all discarded vegetable trimmings from other meals. Collect and keep them in a covered container in the fridge over 2–3 days if you don't have enough on a day-to-day basis. Include left-over cooked vegetables too.

2. Put these trimmings in a pan and cover to twice their height with water, or better still with vegetable water or cooked bean stock (p. 30). Add a whole head of garlic (trimmed) and a few sprigs of herbs (sage, marjoram, parsley etc.), bring to the boil and then simmer for about 1 hour.

3. Strain off the liquid and throw away the solids or put them on your "organic" compost heap. The stock is ready to use immediately or, after cooling, you can keep it in the fridge. We generally cook our stock while we

eat our main meal (using any left-overs from it) and refrigerate it in a screw-top jar to use the next day.

4. Sometimes you may wish to adjust your stock for extra delicate flavour or colour. Carrots, marrows and sweet potatoes give a sweeter flavour. Turnips and sprouts impart their powerful flavour. Onion skins add a golden colour and beetroots a deep pink. Trimmings from celery enhance all the flavours.

5. If you are in a hurry and have no stock ready, don't panic! Substitute it with a little Vecon stirred into boiling water. Taste to check for flavour and seasoning.

FRESH VEGETABLES

Some fresh vegetables should be included in every soup. However unless you are specifically making a mixed vegetable soup, limit your choice to one or two vegetables as the main ingredients of the soup. Most vegetables will make an excellent soup.

If using onions, garlic and spices in your soup, sauté them first in a heavy pan, lightly greased with ghee, for about 10 minutes before adding any other vegetables, seasoning and stock.

THICKENING

There are many ways of creating thicker, more substantial soups. Choose from the suggestions below, each of which can become an integral part of your soup.

1. Include potatoes among your ingredients as they will thicken a soup when they are well cooked.

2. Add cooked left-over grains – rice, millet, wheatgrain.

3. Or add cooked beans – p. 30 – (about 8 oz / 225g / 1½ cups with 1 lb/450g/4 cups of diced vegetables).

4. Or add any other left-over vegetables, puréed.

5. Or add cooked pasta.

6. Add tahini and "silken" or soft tofu for a creamy soup.

7. Make a roux with 5 tbsp wholewheat flour stirred into 2-3 tbsp hot ghee before adding 1 pt, (550ml, 2½ cups) *cold* stock, bringing to the boil and stirring so that it thickens.

8. Use brown rice flour or arrowroot (2 tbsp to each pint of liquid), or a combination of the two mixed to a paste with a little cold water or stock before adding to the simmering soup.

9. Or break 1-2 eggs into a double boiler or - into a saucepan inside another which contains boiling water -, mix with a little brown rice flour or wholewheat flour and stir until thick; then add stock and vegetables.

SEASONINGS

Seasonings are discussed generally in Chapter 2, p. 25 with regard to salt and sugar substitution. As far as soups are concerned, we try to include one small onion per person regardless of the soup. We also use many varieties of peppers, but limit the use of very hot ones to once a week.

We always sauté garlic, onions and spices first if they are included in a recipe. This enhances their flavour. Next we add spirulina or kelp (for salty flavour) and herbs.

Brewer's yeast, nutritional yeast or miso are added when the soup is no longer on the boil, just before serving, to conserve more of their nutrients (p. 26, 185).

PRESENTATION

A swirl of yoghurt, a floating sprig of mint, or a sprinkling of chopped chives will transform the simplest of soups into an eye-catching dish.

Home-made crispbreads (p. 71), breadsticks (p. 69) and hot garlic bread are delicious accompaniments.

Garlic Bread

Cut a wholewheat "French" stick in half horizontally and spread the cut surfaces with butter, blended with crushed garlic and finely chopped fresh parsley. Reassemble your loaf and cut vertically this time, into slices, not quite cutting right through to your bread board. Place your sliced bread in an oven dish and cover with a lid. Bake in a hot oven (gas 6, 200°C, 400°F) for 10–15 minutes. Remove the lid and bake for a further 3–5 minutes.

VEGETABLE SOUPS

Some of our vegetable soup recipes follow, but bearing in mind all the above secrets of successful soup-making you can make whatever soup you choose. You might like to create your own concoctions with some of our favourite combinations of vegetables:

..... watercress, and onion blended when cooked, and served with a swirl of goats' yoghurt (p. 37);

..... young nettles cooked in goat milk seasoned with marjoram and blended;

..... fennel, garlic, celery and ginger, cooked in large chunks, processed and strained – served with a swirl of Tamari on the surface;

..... sorrel and parsley, cooked and then blended, served with 1 tsp quark;

..... broccoli, ground toasted sesame seeds and miso (added just before serving);

..... Jerusalem artichokes, celeriac and thyme, cooked and then blended;

..... beetroot, carrot and onion, cooked and blended and then served with a swirl of goat yoghurt and topped with a sprinkling of parsley;

..... cooked mixed dried beans (p. 30) and pot barley with
  cumin and coriander;
..... yellow peas, artichokes, carrots, onions, thyme and
  oregano, cooked and then blended to a thick, creamy
  soup;
..... chilled cucumber, tofu or yoghurt or a combination,
  and dill weed;
..... carrot and yoghurt thickened with egg (no. 9, of
  Thickeners, p. 95);
..... cooked haricots (p. 30), carrots, leeks and celery cooked
  with goat milk and parsley and then blended;
..... sweet corn, potatoes and goat milk, cooked and then
  blended;
..... mushroom, ginger and pot barley, thickened with
  brown rice flour (p. 95) and garnished with watercress;
..... leeks and potatoes with soya or goat milk, cooked,
  blended and served with a sprinkling of nutmeg.

Thick Split Pea Soup
Preparation time 1¼ hours   *(serves 4)*

    8 oz (225g, 1 cup) dried split peas
    2 pt (1.1 litres, 5 cups) stock (p. 93)
    1 bay leaf
    2 leeks, sliced thinly
    1 onion, chopped
    4 carrots, chopped
    3 sticks of celery
    extra stock if necessary
    seasoning – 1 tsp brewer's yeast, ¼ tsp kelp

Wash and drain the dried peas making sure you get rid of any
small stones, grit etc. Put in a saucepan with the stock and
bay leaf and bring to the boil. Meanwhile prepare the
vegetables (p. 33). Sauté them lightly in a heavy pan brushed
with ghee. Stir them in with the split peas, adding more stock
if necessary, season and simmer on a low heat for about 1
hour. Stir occasionally and check the seasoning. Remove the
bay leaf. Mash with a fork or process for a smoother soup.
Serve piping hot with chunks of warm bread. Will freeze well
or keep for 1–2 days in a covered container in the fridge.

Mulligatawny Soup
Preparation time 1½ hours   *(serves 4)*

  2 tbsp ghee
  1 tsp powdered turmeric
  ½–1 tsp ground chillies
  1 tsp ground coriander
  1 tsp ground cumin
  ½ tsp ground ginger
  3 cloves of garlic, crushed
  4 onions, chopped
  2 carrots, chopped
  1 stick of celery
  2 large eating apples, sliced (and cored though not
     necessary)
  2 pt (1.1 litres, 5 cups approx.) vegetable stock (p. 93)
  2 lemons cut in wedges

Heat the ghee in a heavy pan, add the spices and crushed
garlic and cook gently for 5 minutes, stirring from time to
time. Meanwhile prepare the vegetables and apples (p. 33)
and add these to the spices. Cook together for a further 5
minutes, stirring constantly. Pour in the stock and bring to
the boil. Cover the pan, lower the heat and simmer for at
least an hour. Check the liquid level from time to time,
adding more stock if the soup becomes too thick. It should
be thick but still fluid. Taste for correct seasoning. Cool
slightly and then liquidise or process until smooth. Re-heat
and serve piping hot with wedges of lemon. Will freeze or
keep in a covered container in the fridge for 1–2 days.

* For an even thicker soup, add 4 oz (110g, ¾ cup) cooked,
mashed butter beans, haricots or chick peas before leaving
the soup to simmer for an hour.

Classic French Onion Soup
Preparation time 30 mins.   *(serves 4)*

  6 medium-sized onions
  ghee

2 pt (1.1 litres, 5 cups) vegetable stock (p. 93)
   (a little dry white wine could be included)
1 bay leaf
seasoning – a little yeast extract, Vecon, black pepper

12 thin slices wholewheat (organic) bread
4 oz (110g, 1 cup) grated vegetarian cheese

Peel and slice the onions as thinly as possible. Heat a heavy frying pan gently and brush it lightly with ghee. Sauté the sliced onions until soft and golden. Transfer them to a larger saucepan, add the stock, (and wine if you are using it) and bay leaf, season and bring to the boil. Simmer for 15 minutes. Remove the bay leaf. Toast the slices of bread and warm large heavy china or pyrex serving bowls at the same time. Put two slices in each bowl and ladle your soup over the toasts. They will rise to the surface. Sprinkle them liberally with the grated cheese and place the bowls under the grill. Directly the cheese has melted, serve. The soup itself can be made in advance and stored either in the freezer or in the fridge in a covered container for 1–2 days.

* An alternative to cheese is grated firm tofu with a sprinkling of nutmeg, or a swirl of yoghurt (p. 37) beaten with an egg.

Minestrone
Preparation time 1¼ hours   *(serves 4)*

1 lb (450g, 4 cups) diced mixed vegetables (onions,
   tomatoes, mushrooms, celery, carrots, green beans,
   cooked haricot beans)
ghee
2 pt (1.1 litres, 5 cups) stock (p. 93), preferably a
   tomato-based stock
1 bay leaf
1 oz (25g, ¼ cup) wholewheat macaroni
seasoning – 1 tbsp nutritional yeast flakes, ¼ tsp kelp
   and a sprinkling of black pepper

Wash the vegetables (p. 33) and dice them finely. Heat a

large heavy pan and grease it liberally with ghee. Add all the vegetables and sauté them for about 15 minutes until soft. Onto these vegetables pour the stock and add the bay leaf and the wholewheat macaroni. Bring to the boil and then lower the heat and simmer for 45 minutes. Add more stock if your soup is not as thin as you like it. Remember to check the seasoning. Remove the bay leaf. Serve piping hot. Minestrone will freeze or keep well in the fridge for 1–2 days.

Sally's Vegetable Broth
Preparation time 40 mins.   *(serves 4)*

   2 medium-sized onions
   2 cloves garlic (crushed)
   ghee
   4 oz (110g, 1 cup) washed and diced green beans and
      celery
   4 oz (110g, 1 cup) mushrooms (sliced)
   2 pt (1.1 litres, 5 cups) vegetable stock (p. 93)
   3 tbsp Tamari soy sauce
   seasoning – 1 tsp brewer's yeast, ¼ tsp kelp

Peel the onions, slice them finely and sauté them with the garlic in a heavy pan brushed with a little ghee. Steam the diced beans and celery for 5 minutes. Add these to the onions along with the sliced mushrooms. Sauté all these together for 5 minutes before adding the stock, Tamari and seasoning. Bring to the boil, and then simmer for 15 minutes to allow the flavours to merge a little. Serve hot. May be frozen or kept in the fridge for 1–2 days.

Cream of Broccoli
Preparation time 10 mins.   *(serves 4–6)*

   2 lb (900g, 8 cups) broccoli florets
   3–4 tbsp light tahini
   8 oz (225g, 1 cup) soft tofu
   2 pt (1.1 litres, 5 cups) stock (p. 93)
   seasoning – 1 tsp nutritional yeast, ¼ tsp kelp

Wash the broccoli florets (p. 33) and steam them lightly for about 5 minutes. Blend the tahini, tofu and stock together in a liquidiser, processor or blender, and add the steamed broccoli. Continue to blend until smooth and creamy. Check the seasoning. Delicious cold or hot. Will keep for a day in a covered container in the fridge.

Gazpacho
Preparation time 4 hours   *(serves 4)*

  6 tomatoes
  1 cucumber
  1 green pepper
  2 onions
  1 slice wholewheat bread (organic preferably)
  2 pt (1.1 litres, 5 cups) tomato juice
  dash of tabasco or other pepper sauce

Wash the tomatoes and vegetables (p. 33). Chop them finely. Put them into a bowl with the slice of bread at the bottom, pour over the tomato juice, add the dash of pepper sauce and leave covered in the fridge for 3–4 hours. Using a processor or liquidiser, blend all the ingredients together and refrigerate again until time to serve. Should be ice-cold. Will keep in the fridge in a covered container for 1–2 days and will freeze.

Avocado Soup
Preparation time 10 mins.   *(serves 4)*

  2 ripe avocados
  2 pt (1.1 litres, 5 cups) soya or goat milk
  8 fl oz (225ml, 1 cup) soya or goat yoghurt
  seasoning – cayenne pepper

Peel the avocados, remove and discard the stones. Blend with the milk and yoghurt until smooth. Pour into bowls, sprinkle with cayenne pepper and serve immediately.

Chilled Cucumber and Grapefruit Soup

Preparation time 10 mins.   *(serves 3–4)*

2 cucumbers
1 large grapefruit
2 heaped tbsp goat, sheep or soya yoghurt
chopped fresh mint

Wash the cucumbers (p. 33) and peel the grapefruit. In a food processor or liquidiser, blend the cucumber and grapefruit together. Stir in the yoghurt and chill. Sprinkle with chopped mint before serving.

9

MAIN COURSES

MENU PLANNING

A few simple rules may help you create healthy, appetising menus. Try to make sure that each of your meals always includes:

1. Plenty of raw foods.
2. Some form of "whole" unrefined carbohydrate - bread, pasta, rice etc.
3. A small protein dish.

In Chapter 1 we discussed the importance of variety and how a balanced wholefood diet (with as many of the basic foods as possible being organically produced) should go a long way to providing all the necessary vitamins, minerals etc. we require for good health and plenty of energy too. This chapter deals with main dishes and the sauces which may accompany them. Before coming to the recipes, here is what might be a typical menu of recipes drawn from different parts of this book, paying particular attention to presentation and avoiding repetition of colours, textures or main ingredients:

raw starter – carrot and sugar pea salad (p. 75)

protein dish – savoury loaf (p. 116)

accompaniment – onion sauce (p. 138)

vegetables – steamed broccoli, peppered swede,
            roast potatoes (see below) and gravy (p. 139)

dessert – peach cream topped with toasted almonds
          (p. 155)

VEGETABLE ACCOMPANIMENTS

Our accompanying cooked vegetables are mostly steamed, baked or stir-fried in order to conserve most of the nutrients, but roast potatoes are great favourites too.

Roast Potatoes
Preheat oven to gas 7 (220°C, 425°F). Grease a baking tray with ghee. Allow 1 large potato per person, scrub well, dry in a tea-towel and then slice horizontally into two or more slices of about ½" (1½cm) depth. Dry once again. Place on the tray, cut sides down, and brush any other up-facing cut surfaces with more ghee. Bake for 30 minutes, or until crisp and golden.

Stir-Fried Mixed Vegetables
You can stir-fry almost any selection of vegetables. These would make a tasty combination: spring onions, garlic, bean sprouts (home-sprouted, p. 30), sugar peas, mushrooms, celery, sweet peppers, broccoli, carrots, water chestnuts.

Wash all vegetables thoroughly and dice, chop or cut them into bite-size pieces. Peel and chop one spring onion per person if you are going to use them, use the green part too. Put 1 tbsp cold-pressed sesame oil in a wok, heat and then add your vegetables.

Stir continuously as you add each vegetable. Pay attention to the cooking time of each; for example carrots need a few seconds longer than bean sprouts so they must go in first. More solid ingredients need seconds longer than watery soft items like peppers and mushrooms.

* Delicious with added grated fresh root ginger and a little Tamari soy sauce. To make a complete main meal dish on its own, add extra protein in the form of almonds, seeds, chunks of firm tofu or tempeh (p. 185). Serve on a bed of whole brown rice with a sweet and sour sauce, p. 140 (following sweet corn soup).

* Stir-fried vegetables also make a tasty addition to a soufflé or a savoury pancake filling.

STEWS AND CASSEROLES

Lentil Hotpot
Preparation time 1½ hours   *(serves 6)*

    6 oz (170g, 1 cup) whole green lentils
    6 oz (170g, 1 cup) whole organic brown rice
    3 pt (1½ litres, 7½ cups) boiling water
    2 carrots (sliced)
    1 leek (sliced)
    1 turnip (diced)
    4–6 medium potatoes (1½ between two people)
    2 tsp Tamari soy sauce
    2 tbsp tomato purée
    seasoning – Vecon, brewer's yeast and kelp to taste
    extra stock if necessary
    2 onions
    ghee
    1 handful of fresh parsley (chopped)
    1 tsp dried thyme

Wash the lentils and rice, put them in a saucepan and cover with the boiling water. Bring back to the boil, cover with a lid and then simmer until soft, about 40 minutes. Whilst they are cooking, wash the other vegetables (p. 33) except the onions and potatoes, slice or dice them all and steam lightly for about 5 minutes. Scrub the potatoes, slice them thinly and then steam them too for about 10 minutes in a separate saucepan. The food processor does this slicing well! When the lentils and rice are cooked, remove them from the heat and process half of them with the soy sauce, tomato purée, Vecon, brewer's yeast and kelp to a gravy consistency. You may need to add more liquid (water or vegetable stock) at this stage if the mixture is too dry. Stir the rest of the lentils and rice mixture into the gravy. Peel and chop the onions. Heat a heavy frying pan and brush it with ghee. Sauté the onions in the pan until they become translucent. Pour the lentil and rice mixture into a large casserole dish, add the steamed vegetables, onions and the herbs and adjust the seasoning. Top with the sliced, steamed potatoes. Brush lightly with ghee and bake for 40 minutes at gas 5 (190°C, 375°F). Will keep in the fridge for up to 2 days and freezes well.

* Delicious hot or cold, and any small left-over makes a tasty spread if processed! (You can alter the flavour of a "left-over's" pâté by adding a little mustard, horseradish, tahini etc.)

* Serve with lightly cooked sprouts (following a swede and nasturtium leaf salad in a vinaigrette dressing as a starter – steam thin slices of swede, add the dressing and chill).

* This lentil and rice mixture can be used as a substitute for minced meat in all your favourite recipes such as shepherd's pies and pasta dishes.

Winter Stew
Preparation time 2 hours   *(serves 4–6)*

   4 onions
   1 small celeriac
   ghee
   4 cloves of garlic
   1 lb (450g) seitan or gluten (p. 184)
   2 leeks
   2 carrots

1 small turnip
2 pt (1.1 litres, 5 cups) vegetable stock (p. 93)
2 tsp Vecon or yeast extract
black pepper

Preheat the oven at gas 3 (160°C, 325°F). Wash and prepare
the vegetables (p. 33), peeling only the onions and celeriac.
Brush an oven casserole dish with a little ghee in which to
sauté the vegetables first or alternatively sauté in a separate
frying pan. Crush the garlic, slice the onions and sauté them
for 10 minutes. Add the seitan and continue to cook for a
further 5 minutes, stirring occasionally, while you chop the
remaining vegetables. Add all these to the pan and stir well.
Transfer to your oven casserole dish if you have been using a
frying pan. Pour in the stock, add the seasoning and Vecon.
Stir again and cover with a lid. Place the casserole in the
oven and cook slowly for at least 1½ hours. Will keep for 2
days in a covered container in the fridge or in the freezer.

* Delicious with *Dumplings:*

4 fl oz (110ml, ½ cup) soya or goat's milk
1 tbsp cold-pressed corn oil
1 tsp malt
1 egg
5 oz (140g, 1 cup) maizemeal
1 rounded tbsp wholewheat flour (organic)
1 tsp baking powder (p. 146)

Combine all the wet ingredients in a processor or mixer. Add
this liquid mixture to the remaining ingredients and form a
soft dough, adding a little more flour if the mixture is very
tacky. Break off small pieces and shape into balls. Twenty
minutes before a casserole is due to finish cooking, drop the
dumplings into it and return it to the oven with the lid back
on. Leave to simmer for at least 20 minutes until cooked.
Dumplings do not keep well and are best enjoyed freshly
cooked.

* Delicious with baked jacket potatoes and Savoy cabbage
(following a tomato vinaigrette (p. 80) as starter).

Aduki Stew with Buckwheat and Parsley Dumplings

(serves 6)
Preparation time 1½–2 hours plus soaking overnight

8 oz (225g, 1¼ cups) aduki beans, uncooked
water
1¼ lb (560g) onions
4 carrots
2 parsnips
1 medium swede
1 tbsp ghee
2 pt (1.1 litres, 5 cups) vegetable stock (p. 93)
1 tbsp cider vinegar
1 tsp brewer's yeast
1 bay leaf
1 strip of wakame, about 6"/15cm approx.

Rinse and then soak the aduki beans overnight. Throw away the soaking water, rinse again and cover well with fresh water. Bring to the boil, cook rapidly for 10 minutes and then simmer for about 45–50 minutes until cooked, checking the water level from time to time to make sure it does not boil dry. Peel and chop the onions and wash (p. 33) and then dice the carrots, parsnips and swede. Heat a heavy pan and brush it well with ghee. Sauté the onions until translucent and then toss in the other vegetables and cook together for 5 minutes. Add the stock, cider vinegar, brewer's yeast, bay leaf, wakame and the cooked aduki beans. Bring to the boil and then simmer on a lower heat for at least 45 minutes. Twenty minutes before cooking is complete, remove the bay leaf and wakame, and add the dumplings. Will keep up to 2 days in a covered container in the fridge and freezes well.

Buckwheat and Parsley Dumplings

8 oz (225g, 1½ cups) buckwheat flour
2 tsp baking powder (p. 146)
2 tbsp chopped parsley
2 tbsp oil – cold-pressed sesame or corn
cold water and 1 tsp of lemon juice to bind

Mix the flour, baking powder and parsley together. Fork in
the oil and then slowly add sufficient water and lemon juice
to form a dough. Roll into balls and drop into the casserole
to cook for 20 minutes as above.

* This makes a hearty camping meal served with whole
brown rice and steamed green beans (following a soy slaw (p.
79) as a starter).

PASTA DISHES

Spinach and mushroom Lasagne
Preparation time 1½ hours   *(serves 6)*

   10 strips of wholewheat lasagne, organic
   olive oil
   2 medium onions
   2 cloves of garlic
   4 oz (110g, 1 cup) sliced mushrooms
   1 pepper
   3 tbsp chopped parsley
   3 tsp basil
   3 tsp marjoram
   3 tbsp tomato purée
   2 pt (1.1 litres, 5 cups) vegetable stock (p. 93)
   1 lb (450g) fresh spinach
   1½ lb (675g) firm tofu

Cook the lasagne in plenty of boiling water for about 10
minutes. Drain and lay out on a clean towel to prevent
sticking.

Sauce: Gently heat a heavy pan, greased liberally with olive
oil. Peel and chop the onions, crush the garlic and sauté them
together in the pan. Wash the mushrooms, pepper, and
parsley. Chop these and add them to the onions. Stir well
and cook for 10 minutes. Add the basil, marjoram, tomato
purée and stock, bring to the boil and then simmer for 45
minutes.

Preheat the oven at gas 4 (180°C, 350°F) towards the end of the cooking time for the sauce. Wash the spinach thoroughly, break it into small pieces and steam lightly for about 3 minutes. Mash the tofu and mix it with the spinach. Grease an ovenproof dish by brushing it with olive oil and spoon in a little of the made-up tomato sauce. Add a layer of lasagne followed by a layer of the spinach, and another layer of lasagne followed by the rest of the tomato sauce. Bake for 30–40 minutes. Serve piping hot. Freezes well and will keep up to 2 days in the fridge.

* Delicious with wholewheat garlic bread (p. 96) and a variety of green salads, (following a grilled grapefruit as a starter, p. 92).

Alternatives

..... Use green spinach lasagne with a white lemon sauce (p. 140) and include cashews and grated organic or unsprayed lemon rind for a tangy flavour.

..... Substitute the tomato sauce with a lentil and brown rice gravy. Adapt from the lentil hotpot recipe on p. 105, using sautéed onions, tomatoes and garlic rather than the other vegetables. Top this variation with grated cheese or 4 oz (110g) goat yoghurt whisked up with an egg, and return to oven or grill to brown.

Quick and Easy Spaghetti Bolognese
Preparation time 30 mins.   *(serves 6)*

   1 lb (450g, 2 cups) onions
   2 sticks of celery
   1 tbsp ghee
   12 oz (340g, 1½ cups) split red lentils
   1 pt 6 fl oz (750ml, 3¼ cups) vegetable stock (p. 93)
   2 tbsp tomato purée
   2 bay leaves
   1 tbsp cider vinegar
   1 tbsp dried basil
   1 tsp powdered cinnamon

½ tsp kelp
1–2 tsp brewer's yeast
1 lb (450g) wholewheat spaghetti, organic
olive oil
grated cheese (optional)

Sauce: Peel and chop the onions. Wash and chop the celery
(p. 33). Heat the ghee in a large heavy frying pan and sauté
the onions and celery together for a few minutes. Add all the
remaining sauce ingredients and bring to the boil. Cover the
pan, lower the heat and simmer the sauce for about 15
minutes, stirring occasionally. Add extra stock or water if
the mixture becomes too thick.

Cook the spaghetti in plenty of boiling water for about 20
minutes. Drain, add a little olive oil and toss well. Place the
spaghetti in a large serving bowl, top with the sauce and a
light sprinkling of grated cheese (optional). The sauce will
keep well in either fridge or freezer. The pasta is best eaten
freshly cooked although chilled left-overs make delicious
salads, dressed in a garlic vinaigrette.

* Delicious with steamed broccoli and steamed kohl rabi
(following a grated cabbage salad in a cashew mayonnaise p.
78 as a starter.)

Bean and Pasta Bowl
Preparation time 1½ hours   *(serves 6)*

3 oz (85g, ½ cup) blackeye beans (uncooked,
    p. 30, p. 33)
2 oz (55g, ⅓ cup) flageolets (uncooked, p. 30, p.33)
1 lb (450g) wholewheat pasta shells, organic
2 red onions
2 spring onions
1 green pepper
4 oz (110g, 1 cup) mushrooms
2 sticks of celery
3 medium tomatoes
1 tsp marjoram
1 tsp basil
mustard vinaigrette dressing (p. 86)

Rinse the beans and flageolets and cook separately according to instructions on p. 30. Cook the pasta shells in plenty of water for about 10 minutes. While they are cooking, peel and chop the onions finely, wash and chop the pepper, mushrooms, celery and tomatoes. Drain the beans when cooked, keeping the stock for future use in a soup etc. Combine the cooked beans and pasta shells with the herbs and prepared vegetables in a serving bowl. Toss well in the mustard vinaigrette dressing. Cover and chill for at least 30 minutes before serving. Will keep up to 2 days in the fridge but does not freeze well.

Another time, try adding chopped hard-boiled eggs and a few gherkins to your bowl or alternatively sauté all the vegetables, mix with the cooked beans and pasta, toss in a tsp of olive oil and serve warm.

* Any version is delicious with broccoli, lightly steamed and served in a creamy horseradish sauce – hot or chilled (following an avocado and grapefruit salad as a starter).

Noodle Bake
Preparation time 45–50 mins.   *(serves 6)*

3 eggs
12 oz (340g) wholewheat tagliatelle, organic
4 fl oz (110ml, ½ cup) light tahini
1½ lb (675g) tofu
16 fl oz (450ml, 2 cups) water
juice and rind of 1 lemon (only use the rind if the lemon is unsprayed or organic)
seasoning – nutritional yeast, black pepper
2 tbsp chopped parsley
4 oz (110g, 1 cup) wholewheat breadcrumbs
2–3 tbsp ghee

Preheat the oven at gas 4 (180°C, 350°F). Grease an oven-to-table dish. Hard boil the eggs. Cook the tagliatelle in plenty of boiling water for about 10 minutes until soft and drain. While the eggs and noodles are boiling, you can be blending the tahini, tofu, water, lemon juice, lemon rind and seasoning together in a large mixing bowl. Shell and chop the hard-boiled eggs when ready and fold them into this sauce with the chopped parsley. Add the tagliatelle and spoon the mixture into your prepared oven-to-table dish. Toast the breadcrumbs in a pan which has been liberally greased with ghee and sprinkle them over the tagliatelle mixture. Bake for 30 minutes and serve hot or cold. Will keep up to 2 days in a covered container in the fridge but does not freeze successfully.

* Delicious served with steamed diced mixed root vegetables and boiled new potatoes (following a green spinach and red onion salad, p. 76 as a starter).

BURGERS, RISSOLES AND PATTIES

Brazil Rissoles
Preparation time 1½ hours   (makes approx. 10 rissoles)

   6 oz (170g, 1 cup) brazils, ground
   10 oz (280g, 2 cups) sunflower seeds
   10 oz (280g, 1¼ cups) onions
   1 lb (450g, 4 cups) fresh wholewheat breadcrumbs
   1-2 eggs (optional)
   2 level tbsp tomato purée
   4 tsp dried sage
   1 tbsp dried thyme
   seasoning – brewer's yeast, kelp
   vegetable stock (p. 93)
   ghee for cooking

Grind the nuts and seeds. Peel and chop the onions as finely as possible. Combine all the ingredients together in a saucepan, add sufficient stock to make a firm dough, cover with a saucepan lid or a clean moist tea-towel and leave to stand in a cool place for at least an hour. Heat a heavy pan, and lightly brush it with ghee. Break off pieces of dough about 4 oz (110g) in weight and form rissoles. Place in the hot pan and cook for 10 minutes taking care not to burn

them. Turn and brown the other side. They keep well both in
the fridge and the freezer.

* Delicious with blackcurrant jelly, baked potatoes, parsnips, buttered kale, and gravy (following a sweet carrot
salad as a starter, p. 76).

Tofu Nut Patties
Preparation time 1¼ hours					*(20 patties)*

3 tbsp parsley
1 lb (450g, 2½ cups) walnuts, chopped
8 oz (225g, 1 cup) chopped onions
12 oz (340g) firm tofu
1–2 cloves of garlic, crushed
3 tsp thyme
1 tbsp lemon juice and grated rind of 1 lemon
    (only use the rind if unsprayed; scrub it first)
6 rounded tbsp brown rice flour
2 oz (55g, ½ cup) wheatgerm
stock (p. 93)

Wash the parsley. Chop it and then combine it in a mixing
bowl with the chopped walnuts and onions. Blend the tofu,
garlic, thyme and lemon. Spoon into the nut mixture.
Finally stir in the flour and wheatgerm. Mix well, adding a
little stock if necessary to achieve a dough moist enough to
bind together. Cover the bowl with either a lid or moist clean
tea-towel and leave the dough to stand for about 30 minutes.
    Heat the oven at gas 4 (180°C, 350°F). Grease a baking
tray with ghee. Form patties with the dough, place them on
the baking tray in your hot oven and cook for 30–35 minutes,
turning them over after 15 minutes. These keep up to 2 days
in a fridge and freeze moderately well.

* Delicious with parsley sauce (p. 137–8), sautéed potatoes,
carrots, and mushrooms (following a tossed green salad as a
starter)

Savoury Burgers

Burgers can be easily made by combining nuts, cooked beans or peas with potatoes or cooked grains, onions, herbs or spices and binding the mixture together with tofu, eggs or tahini.

Preparation time 1½ hours   *(serves 4-6)*

ghee
1 onion
1 clove of garlic
1 lb (450g, 3 cups) cooked beans (aduki, chick peas, soya beans etc., p. 30)
2 potatoes, unpeeled, washed, sliced, steamed for 5–10 mins.
large handful of parsley
¼ tsp ground mace
juice and grated rind of 1 lemon (only use the rind if the lemon is unsprayed; scrub it first)
1 tbsp tomato ketchup (p. 142), Tamari soy sauce or a little of each
1 egg, beaten with a little goat or other milk
sesame seeds

Heat a heavy frying pan brushed lightly with ghee. Peel and chop the onion, peel and crush the garlic and sauté both together. Mash the beans and potatoes in a large bowl, add the parsley, mace, lemon juice, grated lemon rind and tomato ketchup and/or Tamari soy sauce. Mix well. Add the sautéed onion and garlic. Taste to check the flavour and adjust if necessary. Press the mixture together to form a ball and leave in the bowl, covered, to stand in a cool place for about an hour if you have the time.

Heat the heavy pan again greased with a little more ghee. Break off suitable pieces and shape them into burgers; dip these in the beaten egg, coat them in sesame seeds and fry each one until golden brown. They keep up to 2 days in the fridge and freeze well.

* Delicious with white onion sauce (p. 138), steamed mixed root vegetables, Brussels sprouts and sautéed potatoes (following a fresh celery, beetroot and apple salad).

SAVOURY LOAF AND ROAST

Simone's Seed Loaf
Preparation time 1–1¼ hours   *(serves 6)*

ghee
12 oz (340g, 1½ cups) finely chopped onions
1 lb (450g, 3¼ cups) sunflower seeds
1 lb (450g, 4 cups) wholewheat breadcrumbs
spirulina
1 tbsp mixed herbs
8 oz (225g, 2 cups) carrots
2 eggs
vegetable stock (p. 93)

Heat a heavy pan, brushed lightly with ghee, and sauté the onions until translucent. Finely process or grind the sunflower seeds and put them in a mixing bowl with the breadcrumbs, seasoning (spirulina) and mixed herbs. Wash the carrots (p. 33) and grate them into the seed mixture. Beat the eggs and stir them in, together with the sautéed onions. Squeeze the mixture in your hands into a firm ball. It should be moist but not wet. Should the consistency require it, add a little stock until it's just right. Place back in the bowl, cover and leave to stand in the fridge for 30 minutes.

Heat the oven at gas 5 (190°C, 375°F). Compress the mixture into one 2 lb (900g) loaf tin greased with ghee and bake for 45 minutes. Cool slightly in the tin before inverting onto a serving platter. Will keep up to 3 days in the fridge and freezes well.

* Delicious with horseradish sauce (p. 141), roast potatoes (p. 104), baked onions, and Savoy cabbage (following a beetroot and apple salad as a starter).

Walnut Roast/Christmas Roast
Preparation time 1¼ hours   *(serves 10)*

6 medium onions
ghee

4–6 sticks of celery
1 medium green pepper
1¾ lb (790g, 6 cups) ground walnuts
1¾ lb (790g, 7 cups) fresh wholewheat breadcrumbs
1 tbsp fresh, chopped chervil
1 tbsp fresh, chopped parsley
1 tsp kelp
2 tsp brewer's yeast
2 eggs

Peel the onions and chop them finely. Heat a heavy pan greased lightly with ghee. Sauté the onions in the pan. Wash the celery and green pepper (p. 33) and chop them as finely as possible. Add them to the onions and toss well together. Transfer to a large mixing bowl, add the ground walnuts, breadcrumbs, chervil, parsley and seasoning (kelp and brewer's yeast). Beat the eggs and add to the nut mixture. Knead lightly together to form a ball. Cover the mixture and leave to stand in a cool place for at least 30 minutes. (We find that leaving the mixture to stand before baking makes a more "sliceable" nut roast.) Transfer the mixture into a large greased bread tin (4 lb/approx. 1½ kilos). Heat the oven at gas 5 (190°C, 375°F). Roast for about 45 minutes. Leave to cool slightly in the tin before inverting onto a large platter. Keeps well in the fridge for 2 to 3 days and freezes well.

* Delicious served with apple sauce, gravy (p. 139), new potatoes, greens and carrots (following chilled grapefruit as starter).

* Try other combinations of nuts. Use equal amounts of nuts and breadcrumbs. If using Brazil nuts, you may find the addition of eggs unnecessary when binding the mixture, as Brazil nuts are very moist.

* For Christmas and special occasions choose a mixture of cashew nuts and sweet chestnuts, use more nuts than breadcrumbs (3 : 1) and substitute dried sage for the chervil in the above recipe.

OVEN-BAKED DISHES

Cauliflower Bake
Preparation time 1 hour   *(serves 8)*

> ghee
> 2 tbsp arrowroot
> 1 tbsp soya flour
> black pepper to taste
> 3 eggs, separated, free-range and organic
> 16 fl oz (450ml, 2 cups) vegetable stock (p. 93) or water
> 2 medium cauliflowers
> 1 lb (450g) spinach
> ½ tsp grated nutmeg
> 8 oz (225g, 1½ cups) broken walnuts

Preheat the oven at gas 5 (190°C, 375°F). Grease a large
ovenproof dish (12″ × 8″/30cm × 20cm) with ghee. Make a
white sauce by blending the arrowroot, soya flour, seasoning
and egg yolks together with the stock or water. Pour this into
a pan and, stirring continuously, cook over a gentle heat
until the resulting sauce thickens. Put aside.

Wash the cauliflowers and spinach (p. 33). Break the
cauliflowers into small florets and steam lightly for 3 to 5
minutes or until they are barely cooked but still crisp. Heat a
heavy saucepan brushed lightly with ghee and break the
spinach into it in small pieces, with a liberal sprinkling of
nutmeg. Cover and cook for 5 minutes. Fork the cauliflower
florets into smaller pieces. Whisk the egg whites until soft
peaks form. Combine the cauliflower, half of the chopped
walnuts and all the white sauce and fold in the beaten egg
whites. Sprinkle the base of the dish with half of the
remaining ground walnuts; spoon on a layer of cauliflower
walnut mixture, followed by the spinach, then the rest of the
cauliflower walnut mixture and, finally, sprinkle the rest of
the ground walnuts on the top. Stand the dish in a deep
baking tray. Pour into the tray enough hot water to reach
three-quarters of the way up the side of the dish and bake for
45 minutes. Will keep up to 2 days in the fridge but does not
freeze well.

* Delicious hot or cold served with stir-fried mixed vegetables, millet cooked in orange juice and a refridgerator relish, p. 144 (following a spicy beetroot salad p. 77).

Baked Stuffed Pancakes
Preparation time approx. 2 hours   *(serves 6–8)*
Make 8–10 thin pancakes

4 oz (110g, ⅔ cup) wholewheat flour
2 eggs
½ pt (300ml, 1¼ cups) goat or soya milk
2 oz (55g) goat or soya yoghurt (optional)
ghee

Measure the flour into a bowl, add the eggs, milk (and yoghurt), and beat well or blend all the ingredients together in a processor or liquidiser. Leave to stand for 30 minutes and beat again if the mixture has separated. Heat a heavy frying pan brushed with ghee and pour in a ladleful of batter or enough to cover the pan thinly; cook until the mixture is set at the centre, toss and brown the other side. Stack in single layers between sheets of greaseproof paper until ready to use.

* Pancakes freeze well between layers of greaseproof paper and packed in polythene bags.

Make two or more fillings:

..... 1 lb (450g) spinach, shredded and lightly stir-fried with a little nutmeg; coat the spinach by stirring in 2 beaten eggs.
..... 12 oz (340g) mushrooms lightly sautéed in a little ghee with 4 oz (110g) finely chopped watercress.
..... 1 lb (450g) Jerusalem artichokes, steamed and then mixed with 2 oz (50g) quark, ½–1 clove of garlic (crushed) and 4 tbsp chopped parsley.
..... 1 lb (450g) sweetcorn kernels puréed in a liquidiser with 2 eggs, and seasoned with a dash of Tamari soy sauce and ½ tsp cumin.

Preheat the oven at gas 6 (200°C, 400°F). Grease a 2 lb (900g) loaf tin with ghee. Line it with crêpes, making sure you cover the corners well. Spoon in half of one filling of your choice; add a layer of crêpes, then a layer of (different) filling; follow by more crêpes and the second half of the first filling. Finally, top off with a layer of crêpes. Cover with a double thickness of greaseproof paper and then foil. Stand immersed three-quarters of the way up the side of the loaf tin in hot water in a baking tray. Cook for 50-60 minutes. Cool slightly in the loaf tin before inverting onto an attractive serving platter. Garnish with watercress and slices of tomato. Keeps up to 2 days in the fridge but does not freeze too successfully.

* Delicious hot with a thick white herby sauce (p. 138) or cold with mayonnaise (p. 87), fresh runner beans and baked potatoes (following cream of broccoli or carrot soup).

Baked Bean and Seitan Cobbler

This is a quick and easy dish to assemble, provided the beans have already been cooked – some planning is necessary though as frozen cooked dried beans do take a while to thaw.

Preparation time 45 mins. *(serves 4)*

    ghee
    2 lb (900g, 6 cups) home-made baked beans (see opposite)
    2 large onions, finely chopped, sautéed
    8 oz (225g) sliced seitan
    8 oz (225g) scone mix: 8 oz (225g) wholewheat flour, 1 tsp baking powder, 2 oz (55g) unsalted butter, 5 fl oz (140ml) milk
    beaten egg yolk mixed with a little goat milk for glazing

Preheat the oven at gas 6 (200°C, 400°F). Grease an oven dish. Spoon in a mixture of baked beans, sautéed onions and seitan and top with scone dough, rolled out and cut into 2″ (5cm) rounds, ½″ (1½cm) thick. Brush these with the beaten egg yolk and goat milk mixture and bake for 20-25 minutes. Serve piping hot. Will keep for 2 or 3 days in the fridge but tends to dry slightly if frozen.

* Delicious with spring greens and turnip in white mustard sauce (following a carrot and raisin salad as starter.)

Baked Beans

(makes approx. 8 lb / 3½ kilos)
Preparation time 6½ hours

* Home-made baked beans are delicious but they do require very long slow cooking. Always make plenty while the oven is on and then freeze them in handy-sized containers.

4 lb (1.8kg, 8 cups) dried haricot beans (uncooked)
water

Rinse and cook the beans (p. 30) until soft but not mushy. Preheat the oven to gas 2 (150°C, 300°F). Divide the beans and their stock between 2 large, greased oven pans which have lids. Top up the liquid by adding enough boiling water to cover the beans well and mix into each panful:

4 fl oz (110ml, ½ cup) apple concentrate
3 tbsp tomato purée
2 tbsp cider vinegar
1 tsp kelp
¼–½ tsp of each: allspice, cinnamon, cayenne

Stir well, put on the lids and bake for about 6 hours. After 3 hours top up with more water or vegetable stock if necessary and check the flavour and seasoning. Cool if not to be used immediately and freeze.

Baked Aubergines
Preparation time 1–1¼ hours   *(serves 6)*

2 large aubergines
sea salt
12 large tomatoes
1 tbsp chopped fresh sweet basil or 1 tsp dried basil
4 tbsp olive oil and for greasing

2 large cloves of garlic, crushed
2 oz (55g, ½ cup) wholewheat breadcrumbs
grated rind of 1 organic or unsprayed lemon
3 oz (75g, ¾ cup) grated vegetarian cheese or
    grated firm tofu mixed with a little nutmeg

Wash the aubergines well (p. 33) and slice them lengthwise.
Place them in a colander, sprinkle with sea salt and leave for
30 minutes. Preheat the oven at gas 6 (200°C, 400°F). Wash
and slice the tomatoes and then wash and chop the sweet
basil. Grease a shallow ovenproof baking dish lightly with
olive oil. Rinse away the sea salt and juices, which will have
oozed from the aubergines, and dry the slices in a clean tea
towel or with kitchen roll. Arrange one layer of aubergines in
the dish, then a thin layer of tomatoes. Mix the basil, oil and
garlic together and sprinkle some of this over the first two
layers. Continue to alternate layers of aubergine, tomato
and the basil and garlic mixture until all the slices of
aubergine and tomato have been used. Mix the breadcrumbs,
lemon rind, and grated cheese or tofu together and sprinkle
evenly over the dish. Bake for 30–45 minutes. Serve piping
hot. Keeps up to 2 days in the fridge and freezes well.

* Try with different toppings from p. 63. Delicious with
steamed broccoli or kale, and baked potatoes (following a
green salad – avoid using olive oil again).

PIES

Sprout and Chestnut Pie

Preparation time 1 hour   *(makes 1 × 10" (25cm) pie)*

Pastry: use twice the amount given in the basic oil pastry
recipe (p. 70). Line the bottom of a greased pie plate with half
of the pastry dough and sprinkle the surface with finely
ground semolina.

Filling

8 oz (225g) chestnuts, fresh

1 lb (450g) Brussels sprouts
2 oz (55g, ¼ cup) ghee or full butter
8 oz (225g, 1 cup) onions, chopped
2 cloves of garlic, crushed
2 tsp basil
1 tsp oregano
2 oz (55g, ⅓ cup) wholewheat flour
1 pt (550ml, 2½ cups) stock or sprout water
2 oz (55g) grated cheese, optional
seasoning of choice – nutritional yeast and black pepper
beaten egg white, for glazing

Preheat oven at gas 6 (200°C, 400°F). Make crosses on the
skins at the flat ends of the chestnuts and plunge them into
boiling water for 5 minutes. Drain and peel when sufficiently
cool. Wash and prepare the sprouts (p. 33). Steam them for
about 5 minutes until they are very lightly cooked. Place the
chestnuts and sprouts in your prepared pastry base. Gently
fry the onions, garlic and herbs together for a few minutes in
a little ghee. Add the flour and mix well to form a roux.
Remove from the heat and add the cool stock, stir well and
then return to the heat to cook until the sauce thickens. Add
the grated cheese if you wish to include it. Pour the sauce
over the sprouts and chestnuts. Season to taste.

Roll out the second half of chilled pastry and top the pie.
Wet and pinch the edges, glaze with beaten egg white and
bake in the preheated oven for about 35 minutes. Delicious
hot or cold. Consume within 2 days or freeze.

Filling Alternatives

Cooked beans make good pie fillers too.

Rinse, soak and then cook 8 oz (225g, 1 cup) beans (p. 30).
The small blackeye is one of our favourites.

Wash and prepare 12 oz (340g) of mixed seasonal
vegetables, slice or dice them and sauté them lightly in a pan
greased with ghee. Mix them with the cooked beans, add
seasoning, herbs or spices and a little bean stock if the
mixture appears too dry. Fill a pastry case as for sprout and
chestnut pie and top with the remaining pastry. Bake for 35
minutes at gas 6 (200°C, 400°F).

Other combinations to experiment with:

..... leeks and lentils, carrots and onions seasoned with
    Tamari soy sauce;
..... aduki beans, apple, sultanas, walnuts and cinnamon;
..... butter beans, grated goats' cheese, mace.

Vegetarian Shepherd's Pie
Preparation time 1¼ hours   *(serves 6)*

   8 oz (225g, 1⅓ cups) whole brown rice
   8 oz (225g, 1½ cups) aduki beans
   2 pt 8 fl oz (1 litre 350ml, 6 cups) boiling water, approx.
   ghee
   4 medium onions
   4 carrots
   1 small swede
   1 small celeriac
   handful fresh parsley
   1 tsp marjoram
   seasoning – 2 tsp brewer's yeast, ½ tsp kelp
   water or vegetable stock (p. 93)
   4 medium potatoes
   grated vegetarian cheese (optional)

Rinse and drain the rice and aduki beans. Soak together for
about half an hour in plenty of boiling water. Drain and then
bring them to the boil with fresh boiling water in a large
saucepan; cover, lower the heat and simmer for about 40
minutes.

Preheat the oven at gas 4 (180°C, 350°F). Heat a heavy
frying pan brushed with ghee. Peel and chop the onions and
sauté them until transparent. Wash and trim the carrots,
swede and celeriac (p. 33), peeling only if the skins appear
very tough. Dice these vegetables and add them to the
onions. Also add the herbs and seasoning.

When the beans and rice are cooked, remove them from
the heat, let them cool slightly in their stock and then process
them into a thick gravy adding more vegetable stock or
water if necessary. Combine the vegetables and gravy and

pour into an oven dish (about 12″ × 8″, 30cm × 20cm)
greased with ghee.

Wash and dice the potatoes and steam them lightly for
about 10 minutes before mashing them. Spread the potato
over the top of the bean mixture and fork roughly. Sprinkle
a little ghee or grated vegetarian cheese over the top and
bake for 45 minutes. Will keep in the fridge up to 2 days and
freezes well.

* Delicious with sautéed mushrooms and Brussels sprouts
(following honeydew melon as a starter).

RICE AND GRAIN DISHES

We eat organic whole brown rice and millet either as our
main dish or as an accompaniment to a main meal about
four times a week.

Cooking Whole Brown Rice

* Remember to allow time. Brown rice takes about 35–45
minutes to cook.

(serves 3–4)

1 lb (450g, 2½ cups) rice
1½ pt (850ml, 3¾ cups) water
   or
for one-two people
1 cup rice to just under 2 cups water

Rinse the rice, drain and put in a large saucepan. Pour in the
water and bring to the boil. Cover with a tightly fitting lid
wrapped in a clean tea towel, securely tied above for safety
from fire, lower the heat to almost the "off" position and
leave for about 40 minutes undisturbed. The rice will absorb
all the water and be dry and nutty in flavour.

Cooking Whole Millet

Follow the same procedure as for the rice but begin by
toasting the millet in a hot, heavy pan liberally greased with
ghee until it has a nutty roasted aroma.

* You can create wonderful variations by adding nuts,
seeds, marinated cubes of firm tofu, tempeh, vegetables
and/or fruits to cooked rice or millet. Serve hot with a sauce
from Chapter 10 (e.g. sweet and sour sauce), or cold with a
mayonnaise (p. 87), either way combined as a meal in itself
with a large but simple green salad and garlic bread, or as
part of another main dish.

A few more ideas follow for cold protein dishes or hot fried
rice dishes made from left-over cooked brown rice or millet:

..... add chopped sweet peppers, broken walnut pieces and
       chopped endive;
..... add almonds, grapes, slices of banana dipped in lemon
       juice, and all tossed in a curry mayonnaise (simply add
       curry powder to any mayonnaise to taste, p. 87–90).

Rice Ring

Left-over cooked rice can be turned into a fancy rice ring to
serve cold. Mix cooked rice with chopped peppers, chopped
spring onions, raw peas and sliced mushrooms, toss in a little
ghee or olive oil, then press into a mould and chill in the
fridge overnight.
   Another simple thing to do with uncooked rice or millet is
to create a risotto or millotto into which you can virtually
"throw" your favourite flavours.

Tamarind and Walnut Risotto
Preparation time 50 mins.   *(serves 4–6)*

   1–2 tbsp cold-pressed sesame oil
   4 onions
   12 oz (340g, 2 cups) long grain organic rice (uncooked)
   6 oz (170g, 1½ cups) broken walnut pieces

4 oz (110g, 1 cup) whole button mushrooms
1-2 oz (25-55g) chopped tamarind
1 small sweet red pepper, chopped
a few curry-leaves
1 pt (550ml, 2½ cups) boiling vegetable stock (p. 93)
   or water

garam masala
desiccated coconut

Heat a heavy pan and add the cold-pressed sesame oil. Peel
and slice the onions and sauté them in the oil. Rinse the rice,
add and continue to sauté for 5 minutes. Add the remaining
ingredients except the stock, garam masala and coconut,
stirring them round for even distribution. Carefully pour in
the stock or water. Cover with a tightly fitting lid wrapped in
a clean tea towel, securely tied above for safety from fire.
Simmer for about 40 minutes until all of the liquid has been
absorbed. Serve hot or cold topped with a sprinkling of
garam masala and coconut. Will keep for up to 2 days in the
fridge and freezes satisfactorily.

STUFFED VEGETABLES
AND FRUITS

Stuffed Mushrooms
Preparation time 40 mins.   *(serves 6–8)*

2 medium onions, chopped
ghee
8 oz (225g, 2 cups) coarse wholewheat breadcrumbs
4 oz (110g, 1 cup) chopped walnuts
1 tbsp tomato purée
1 tbsp chopped, fresh parsley
1 tsp dried marjoram
seasoning – brewer's yeast and kelp
1 lb (450g) large open mushrooms

Preheat oven at gas 4 (180°C, 350°F). Peel and chop the

onions and sauté them to a golden brown in a frying pan
lightly greased with ghee. Add the breadcrumbs, nuts,
tomato purée and herbs. Season to taste. Wash the
mushrooms (p. 33) and remove the stalks. Slice the stalks
and add them to the nut mixture. Lightly steam the
mushroom heads for 5–10 minutes. Pile the nut mixture
onto the underside of the mushroom heads and press down
as much as possible. Place the mushrooms in a lidded oven
dish greased with ghee, and pour in a little boiling water at
the bottom. Cover with the lid and cook in the moderate
oven for 30 minutes. Alternatively return to a shallow,
covered pan and poach in a little boiling water for 20–25
minutes.

* Delicious with steamed broad beans, carrot purée,
sautéed potatoes (following a red bean salad, p. 82).

Stuffed Courgettes

Courgettes are delicious sliced lengthwise, hollowed out and
stuffed with chopped, hard-boiled eggs, breadcrumbs,
spinach, mushrooms, green pepper, tomato purée, basil and
oregano. Bake as for the stuffed mushrooms, above.

Stuffed Raw Tomatoes
Preparation time 15 mins.   *(serves 6)*

  12 large tomatoes
  6 oz (170g, 1½ cups) cooked green beans
  6 oz (170g, 1½ cups) cooked flageolets
  2 hard-boiled eggs, chopped
  vinaigrette with 1 tbsp fresh, chopped parsley and
    1 tbsp fresh chopped tarragon

Wash the tomatoes well (p. 33). Cut into halves and scoop
out the flesh. Mash the flesh and combine it with the cooked
beans, chopped hard-boiled eggs and vinaigrette. Pile this
mixture back into the tomatoes and chill in the fridge.

* Delicious served on a bed of green salad with a curried
brown rice salad (following garlic, fennel and ginger soup).

* Tomatoes are particularly tasty when stuffed with chopped walnuts, breadcrumbs, lemon rind and juice, herbs and chopped black olives. This dish may be raw or oven-baked.

SPICY DISHES

Our family has a deep-rooted love of spicy foods. Spices enhance wholefood cookery and together with herbs definitely make the change from highly seasoned modern convenience foods more acceptable for many.

Groundnut Stew
Preparation time approx. 2 hours   *(serves 4–6)*

  1 large onion
  1 clove of garlic
  ¾″ (2cm) dried chilli pepper
  4 large tomatoes
  1 large green pepper
  1 tbsp ghee
  1 lb (450g) firm tofu, frozen, thawed and cubed (p. 185)
  10 oz (280g, 1 cup) peanut butter
  1¼ pt (675ml, 3 cups) water
  10 oz (280g, ½ cup) tomato purée
  2 tbsp chopped fresh parsley
  seasoning – soy sauce, brewer's yeast, kelp

Peel the onion, peel and crush the garlic and finely chop the chilli. Take great care not to touch your face especially your eyes whilst handling the chilli as chilli burns. Wash the tomatoes and pepper thoroughly (p. 33) and chop them. Sauté for about 5 minutes all these ingredients in a large heavy saucepan which has been brushed liberally with ghee. Add the cubes of tofu and continue to sauté for a further 3 minutes.

Mix the peanut butter with a cupful of the water and stir it into the vegetables to distribute it evenly. Now you can add all the other ingredients and bring the stew to the boil. Lower the heat and simmer for at least 1½ hours – the longer you simmer the better the flavour! Will keep up to 3 days in the fridge but does not freeze.

* Delicious served on a bed of brown rice, decorated with slices of hard-boiled egg and complemented by a small vegetable curry, p. 135 (following avocado boats as a starter, p. 91).

The Africans make a groundnut stew with chicken instead of tofu and peanuts (groundnuts) instead of peanut butter.

Marinated Tofu Steaks
Preparation time 40 mins. *(serves 3–4)*

    1 lb (450g) firm tofu
    2 tsp Tamari soy sauce
    1 tsp grated fresh root ginger
    8 fl oz (225ml, 1 cup) water
    ghee

Drain the tofu. Cut into slices ¼″ (½cm) thick. Arrange in a shallow dish. Mix the Tamari, ginger and water together and pour over the tofu slices. Allow to marinate for about 30 minutes. Drain and dab dry with a paper towel. Heat a heavy pan, brush it with a little ghee and put in the slices of tofu. Brown both sides. Will keep in the fridge for a day but does not freeze.

* Delicious with stir-fried broccoli, whole brown rice or millet, and sweet and sour sauce, p. 140 (following a salad of Chinese leaves and home-sprouted alfalfa sprouts as a starter). Tofu steaks are equally delicious in large bread rolls with spicy tomato sauce (p. 143) and any salad of your choice.

* Tofu steaks can be substituted for chicken in some of your own favourite recipes.

Chinese Tofu
Preparation time 10–15 mins.   *(serves 4–6)*

4 onions
1 green pepper
4 oz (110g) broccoli
a few bamboo shoots
1 lb (450g) firm tofu
1 handful of mung bean sprouts
1–2 tbsp cold-pressed sesame oil
1″ (2½cm) fresh root ginger
1 tbsp Tamari soy sauce or to taste

Wash the vegetables (p. 33). Drain and cut the tofu into cubes. Peel and slice the onions, chop the green pepper. Cut the broccoli into small florets and trim the bamboo shoots. Rinse the bean sprouts.

Heat the oil in a wok or heavy pan. Add the onions and sauté until transparent. Add the tofu, bamboo shoots, broccoli, green pepper and mung bean sprouts and stir well. Grate in the ginger and add the Tamari soy sauce. Cook, stirring all the time, for a few minutes; then serve immediately. Does not freeze but any left-overs can be combined with a few fresh ingredients as pancake filling.

* Delicious with whole brown rice and braised or poached celery (following clear garlic and egg soup as a starter).

Try some different tofu steak ideas

1. Marinate in goat yoghurt, flavoured with curry powder; then dip in beaten egg and fry until golden brown.
2. Or dip in beaten egg and coat with wholewheat breadcrumbs; then fry or bake and serve with pineapple and almond sauce (a béchamel sauce (p. 137), substituting some of the liquid with pineapple juice and adding pineapple pieces and toasted almonds).

Dhal
Preparation time 45 mins.   *(serves 4)*

    1 lb (450g, 2 cups) yellow split peas
    2 pt (1.1 litres, 5 cups) water
    ½ tsp chilli powder
    8 oz (225g) tomatoes
    4 medium onions
    ghee
    ½ tsp black mustard seeds
    2 cloves of garlic, crushed
    ¼ tsp turmeric

Rinse the split peas under a running tap, put them into a
saucepan and cover with the water. Add the chilli powder
and bring to the boil. Lower the heat, cover and simmer for
about 25 minutes until tender. Wash the tomatoes and peel
the onions. Slice both. Heat a heavy pan and brush it lightly
with ghee. Add the mustard seeds and cook until they pop.
Then add the onions, crushed garlic, turmeric and tomatoes,
and sauté together for 5 minutes. Combine with the cooked
split peas and continue to cook for a further 10 minutes
adding more boiling water if necessary to retain consistency.
Dhal should be like a thick sauce. It keeps in the fridge for 3
to 4 days and may be frozen.

* Delicious served with boiled whole brown rice, accompanied by Indian breads (p. 68), a small spinach curry and a
small aubergine curry (following a salad of cucumber slices
in yoghurt, sprinkled with mint, as a starter).

Spicy Millotto
Preparation time 50 mins. – 1 hour   *(serves 6)*

    2 tbsp ghee
    ½ tsp ground chilli
    1 tsp ground cumin
    1 tsp ground cardamom seeds
    1 tsp turmeric
    8 oz (225g, 1⅓ cups) uncooked millet, rinsed
    4 oz (110g, 1 cup) chopped mushrooms (pressed firmly
    into cup)

8 oz (225g, 1 cup) chopped onions
4 oz (110g, ²/₃ cup) sultanas (unsulphured, washed)
4 oz (110g, 1 cup) whole almonds
1 tsp brewer's yeast
½ tsp kelp powder
12 fl oz (350ml, 1½ cups) water, boiling

½ small pineapple, sliced
shredded or desiccated coconut

Grease a heavy frying pan with the ghee. Add the spices and cook for 5 minutes. Add the uncooked millet and heat gently with the spices. Add the mushrooms, onions, sultanas, almonds, brewer's yeast and kelp to the millet mixture. Stir together, heating gently for another 2 to 3 minutes. Pour the boiling water over this mixture and cover the pan with a tightly fitting lid. Lower the heat and cook for 30–40 minutes or until all the water has been absorbed and the millet is soft but not mushy. Keeps a day or two in the fridge and may be frozen.

* Delicious served garnished with slices of fresh pineapple and a sprinkling of coconut accompanied by a celery and yoghurt salad, a mixed green salad and a small tomato vinaigrette (following fresh carrot juice as a starter – this can be bought bottled if you do not own a juicer).

* Whole organic brown rice can be substituted for the millet in the above recipe and 2 tsp grated fresh root ginger for the curry spices.

Castaway Cashews
Preparation time 20 mins. *(serves 6)*

1¼ lb (560g) onions
ghee
6 oz (170g, 1½ cups) mushrooms
6 oz (170g, 1⅓ cups) broken cashews
2 large bananas, sliced
3 tbsp desiccated coconut
1 tbsp garam masala

Peel and slice the onions and then sauté in a heated pan, lightly brushed with ghee. Wash and slice the mushrooms (p. 33). Add the mushrooms, cashews and sliced bananas to the onions and sauté all these ingredients for 10 minutes. Transfer this mixture to a warmed serving dish and sprinkle with the coconut and garam masala. Will keep in the fridge for a day but does not freeze.

* Delicious served with braised red cabbage, mango relish and cooked brown rice (following corn-on-the-cob with garlic butter as a starter).

Ben's Savoury Curry Balls
Preparation time 45 mins.   *(serves 4–6)*

    4 oz (110g, 1 cup) green lentils
    1 pt (550ml, 2½ cups) water
    4 medium onions
    ghee
    1 tbsp curry powder
    2 large carrots
    4 oz (110g, 1 cup) wholewheat breadcrumbs
    1 egg
    1 tbsp tomato paste
    sesame seeds

Rinse the lentils, put them in a pan with the water and bring to the boil. Cover the pan with a well-fitting lid, reduce the heat and simmer for about 30 minutes. Meanwhile peel and chop the onions. Heat a heavy frying pan and grease it lightly with ghee. Add the chopped onions and sauté with the curry powder for 10 minutes. Wash and grate the carrots (p. 33). Combine the breadcrumbs, grated carrot, egg and tomato paste in a mixing bowl and stir well. Add the sautéed onion and curry mixture.
    When the lentils are cooked and soft, drain and retain the stock for an accompanying vegetable curry sauce. Process or mash the lentils and then combine with the curry mixture. Mix thoroughly and then press into a large ball (add a little more lentil stock if the mixture is too dry). Break off pieces,

form small balls, roll in sesame seeds and brown uniformly in the frying pan with a little more ghee if you need it. Keep hot in the oven until ready to serve with the following recipe – vegetable curry sauce. These curry balls keep well for up to 2 days in the fridge and will freeze.

Vegetable Curry Sauce
This sauce is quite substantial and could be served as a small vegetable curry.

Preparation time 1 hour   *(4–6 servings)*

1 tbsp ghee
1 tsp of each – turmeric, ginger, cumin, coriander
$\frac{1}{2}$–1 tsp chilli powder
2 very large onions
8–12 medium potatoes
$\frac{1}{2}$ swede
8 oz (225g) green beans
8 oz (225g) carrots
2 oz (55g, $\frac{1}{3}$ cup) raisins, untreated and washed
8 fl oz (225ml, 1 cup) vegetable stock (p. 93)

Heat a heavy pan, brush it liberally with ghee, add the spices and cook for 5 minutes. Peel and chop the onions and add them to the spices. Wash the other vegetables (p. 33).

Dice the potatoes and swede and slice the beans and carrots. Add the vegetables to the onions and spices. Stir well and cook together for 5–10 minutes before adding the raisins and stock. Bring to the boil, reduce the heat and simmer for 45 minutes. Keeps well in the fridge for up to 3 days and will freeze satisfactorily.

* Delicious with brown rice or wholewheat pasta, Indian breads, a dry cauliflower curry and date and apple relish, p. 144 (following a lightly steamed broccoli and raw onion salad).

A dry cauliflower curry is simply made by cooking curry spices in a little ghee, adding small florets of cauliflower and tossing well for 3 to 4 minutes over a gentle heat. This is tasty eaten immediately or chilled.

Falafels
Preparation time 20 mins.   *(serves 3–4)*

   6 oz (170g, 1½ cups) cooked chick peas (p. 30)
   2 oz (50g, ⅓ cup) wholewheat flour
   1 tsp of each – cumin, coriander, sage, thyme
   seasoning – brewer's yeast, kelp
   chick pea stock or water
   ghee

Grind the cooked chick peas in a processor or mash with a
fork and put into a mixing bowl. Add the flour, spices, herbs
and seasoning. Knead and press the mixture into a ball to
test the consistency as you may need to add a little chick pea
stock or water if the mixture does not bind together. Heat a
heavy pan greased with ghee. Form small balls and cook in
the pan, turning regularly until evenly browned.

* Serve in pitta pockets, either hot or cold, with hummus (p.
54) and various small salads (following a chilled cucumber
and grapefruit soup, p. 102).

10

SAUCES

Sauces are the secret of success in vegetarian cuisine. They will transform simple, inexpensive vegetarian meals into specialities of the house.

Béchamel Sauce- the wholefood way
Pepper is an essential ingredient in this sauce.
Preparation time 10 mins.   *(makes a family-size jugful)*

   3 tbsp ghee
   5 tbsp wholewheat flour
   16 fl oz (450ml, 2 cups) cold goat or soya milk
   freshly ground black pepper

Warm the ghee in a heavy saucepan, stir in the flour with a wooden spoon and, when all the ghee has been absorbed by the flour, remove from the heat and add the milk. Return to the heat, season and bring slowly to the boil, stirring continuously to avoid lumps forming. Cook for a further 2 or 3 minutes – the sauce should be thick and creamy. Check the seasoning.

   Some wholewheat flour is more absorbent than others, so be prepared to make adjustments. Never add hot liquids to a roux (the flour and ghee mixture).

Another White Sauce
To cut down on the fat, use brown rice flour when making a basic sauce.
Preparation time 5 mins.   *(makes a family-sized jugful)*

2 tbsp brown rice flour
16 fl oz (450ml, 2 cups) goat or soya milk, or half
    milk and half water
freshly ground black pepper

Mix the brown rice flour and milk together in a pan. Heat
and stir continuously until the mixture thickens and comes
to the boil. Season and use.

Variations On This Theme

Using either of the sauce bases above, adjust as below.

A. Stir into the finished sauce either:
   1. chopped capers and lemon juice after cooking and
      cooling slightly;
or 2. hard-boiled eggs (chopped) and lemon juice;
or 3. ½–1 tsp nutmeg;
or 4. 2–4 tbsp goat or soya yoghurt.

B. Cook the sauce with the addition of:
   1. 2 tsp of each – chopped parsley, chopped chervil,
      chopped tarragon – 1 small onion finely chopped and
      3 tbsp dry white wine (optional);
or 2. 1 small onion (finely chopped) and 4 tbsp finely
      chopped parsley, celery or fennel.

C. Substitute for the liquid in the sauce:
   1. diluted pineapple juice, crushed pineapple and a few
      toasted almonds;
   2. vegetable stock (p. 93) and add 2 oz (55g, ½ cup)
      chopped mushrooms and 1 small onion, chopped;
or 3. *Onion Sauce:* boil a large peeled onion and cook until
      soft; use both the liquid and the onion (chopped)
      with a sprinkling of nutmeg as part of your liquid in
      one of the basic white sauces above.

Béchamel sauce and any of these variations complement
burgers, rissoles and savoury loaves.

Tartare Sauce
Preparation time 3 mins.   *(makes a small jugful)*

    1 handful of spinach
    1 small pickled onion
    2 tbsp capers
    8 fl oz (225ml, 1 cup) egg mayonnaise (p. 87)
    1–2 tsp mustard

Wash the spinach thoroughly (p. 33), steam the leaves for a
minute or two and drain. Squeeze the spinach over a bowl to
collect the green spinach water. Chop 1–2 of the spinach
leaves, the onion and capers. Add to the mayonnaise with a
few drops of the spinach water to colour. Season with
mustard and pepper. Will keep in a screw-top jar for 2 to 3
days in the fridge.

Tartare sauce complements oven-baked tofu steaks and is
delicious with tofu nut burgers.

Brown Gravy
Preparation time 5 mins.   *(makes a family-size jugful)*

    3 tbsp ghee
    5 tbsp wholewheat flour
    16 fl oz (450ml, 2 cups) cold vegetable stock (p. 93)
    ½ tsp kelp
    1 tbsp brewer's yeast
    1 tbsp miso or Vecon

Warm the ghee in a heavy saucepan, add the flour and stir
well to make a roux. Add the stock whilst continuing to stir.
Season to taste with the kelp and brewer's yeast. Bring the
sauce to the boil. (If the sauce is too thick – each batch of
wholewheat flour varies in absorbency from the others – add
more *cold* stock and whisk quickly to avoid lumps forming.
Bring back to the boil.) Simmer the gravy for 3 minutes.
Remove from the heat and allow to cool slightly before
adding the Vecon or miso, and checking these seasonings to
taste before serving.

* Never boil miso – high temperatures kill the invaluable enzymes which are a great aid to our digestive systems.

Brown gravy is an essential addition to any special nut roast or cutlets.

Sweet and Sour Sauce
Preparation time 10 mins.   *(makes a family-size jugful)*

   ghee
   3 medium onions
   1 clove of garlic (crushed)
   6 carrots
   1 green pepper
   4 tbsp date purée
   1 tsp soy sauce
   3 tbsp cider vinegar
   1 pt (550ml, 2½ cups) pineapple juice
   1 tbsp arrowroot mixed to a paste with 1 tbsp water
   ½ small pineapple, cubed

Heat a heavy saucepan and grease it with a little ghee. Peel the onions, chop finely and sauté with the garlic. Wash the carrots and pepper (p. 33) and chop into small pieces. Add them to the onions and cook together for a further 3–5 minutes. Add the date purée, soy sauce, cider vinegar and pineapple juice and bring to the boil. Stir in the arrowroot paste and continue to cook, stirring continuously, until the sauce thickens. Add the pineapple chunks. Keeps well in a screw-top jar in the fridge for about a week. Freezes well.

   Sweet and sour sauce is especially good with pancakes stuffed with stir-fried vegetables.

Lemon Sauce
Preparation time 10 mins.   *(makes a small jugful)*

   2 tbsp brown rice flour
   8 fl oz (225ml, 1 cup) stock or water
   1 tsp pure lemon oil

sprinkling of fresh, grated root ginger
4 tbsp goat yoghurt or other
juice and grated rind of 1 lemon (organic)

Mix the brown rice flour and water or stock together in a
saucepan. Bring gently to the boil, stirring constantly, then
lower the heat and continue to cook until the mixture
thickens. Add the lemon oil and grated ginger. Remove from
the heat, cool slightly and then whisk in the yoghurt and
lemon.

Delicious with tofu steaks and walnut burgers.

Horseradish Sauce
Preparation time 3 mins.   *(makes a small jarful)*

2 tbsp freshly grated horseradish
1 tbsp malt or apple concentrate
1 tbsp cider or white wine vinegar
6 tbsp tofu, firm or silken (p. 185)
2 tsp mustard

Blend all the ingredients together and store in a screw-top jar
in the fridge. Check the seasoning. Will keep for 2 to 3 weeks.

Horseradish sauce complements a good walnut roast.

Mint Sauce
Preparation time 3 mins.   *(makes up 6 tablespoonfuls)*

4 tbsp finely chopped mint
4 tbsp boiling water
1 tbsp cider vinegar
1–2 tbsp date purée
juice of 1 lemon

Wash and chop the mint as finely as possible. Put it in a jug
and pour the boiling water over it. Add the remaining
ingredients and mix well.

Mint sauce complements a sunflower and pumpkin seed
loaf well.

Cranberry and Apple Jelly
Preparation time 25 mins.   (fills 1 × 12 oz/340g jam jars)
Plus 2 hours cooling

8 oz (225g, 1½ cup) cranberries
2 eating apples
1 pt (550ml, 2½ cups) apple juice
1-2 sprigs sweet cicely (optional)
4 tsp agar-agar
1 tbsp raw honey

Wash the cranberries and eating apples (p. 33). Put the cranberries in a saucepan, slice the apples thinly, add them and pour the apple juice over the fruit. Add one or two sprigs of sweet cicely if available. Poach lightly for about 15 minutes and when cooked, remove the herb and sprinkle the agar-agar flakes on the fruit. Stir well, bring to the boil and simmer for 5 minutes. Cool thoroughly and stir in the honey. Pour into a glass dish and refrigerate for about 2 hours. Will keep in the fridge for one to two weeks.

Try this sauce with a chestnut or cashew roast.

Tomato Ketchup
Preparation time 5 mins.   (fills a large screw-top jar)

8 rounded tbsp tomato paste
16 fl oz (450ml, 2 cups) water
8 tsp apple concentrate
8 tsp cider vinegar
1-2 cloves of garlic, crushed
pinch of cayenne pepper
1 tsp of each – kelp, powdered cinnamon, allspice

Combine all the ingredients, mix well, check the seasoning, pour into a large screw-top jar and keep in a refrigerator. Keeps well both in the fridge and freezer.

Tomato ketchup adds colour and flavour to your brunch recipes.

Spicy Tomato Sauce
Preparation time 25 mins.   *(fills a large screw-top jar)*

ghee
2 cloves of garlic, crushed
2 tsp mustard
1 tsp allspice
1–2 tbsp malt or apple concentrate
3 tbsp lemon juice
1 handful of fresh chervil, chopped
3 rounded tbsp tomato paste
8 fl oz (225ml, 1 cup) apple juice

Heat a heavy pan greased with ghee. Sauté the garlic quickly and then add the mustard and allspice. Cook together for 2 minutes. Add the remaining ingredients, stir and bring to the boil. Simmer for 15 minutes on a very low heat. Check the seasoning to taste. Cool and store in a screw-top jar. Keeps well in both fridge or freezer.

Spicy tomato sauce enhances a tofu and millet platter.

Peanut Sauce
Preparation time 40 mins.   *(fills a large screw-top jar)*

ghee
2 onions
1 clove of garlic, crushed
1 tsp grated fresh root ginger
5 tbsp peanut butter
juice of 1 lemon
1½ pt (850ml, 3¾ cups) stock or water
1 tbsp malt
1 tbsp cider vinegar
seasoning – brewer's yeast and kelp

Heat a heavy pan greased with ghee. Peel and chop the onions and sauté with the garlic for 5–10 minutes. Add all the other ingredients, bring to the boil and simmer for 25 minutes. Check the seasoning. Will keep in the fridge for about 3 days and freezes well.

Peanut sauce will complement any nut or seed risotto or millotto and sweet vegetable curries.

Date and Apple Relish
Preparation time 20 mins.   *(fills a large screw-top jar)*

1 lb (450g) chopped dried dates and figs
2 medium onions
4 sharp eating apples
juice and rind of 2 lemons (only use the rind if the
   lemon is unsprayed)
½–1 tsp chilli powder
16 fl oz (450ml, 2 cups) fresh fruit juice – apple
   or orange juice

Wash and drain the dried fruits. Peel and chop the onions and apples as finely as possible. Scrub the lemons, extract the juice and grate the rinds. Put all the ingredients into a pan and bring to the boil. Simmer until the mixture thickens. Check the seasoning. Cool and store for up to 3 weeks in a screw-top jar in the fridge.

* Try other combinations of fresh and dried fruits and spices – dried, unsulphured pineapple, ginger and onion; dates, apples, tomato and allspice; or gooseberries, rhubarb, ginger and onion.

Date and apple relish is delicious with cold meals, rice dishes and with curries.

Refrigerator Relish
                       (fills a large screw-top jar)
Preparation time 10 mins. plus chilling time

6 sticks of celery
2 large green peppers
2 small onions
1 heaped tbsp chopped dates, organic if available
1 heaped tbsp raisins, untreated if available

1 tbsp cider vinegar
1 tbsp cold-pressed sunflower oil

Wash (p. 33), trim and chop all the vegetables as finely as
possible. Mix the vinegar and the oil together and add to the
chopped vegetables. Pour into a clear glass container, cover
and leave in the fridge for at least 2 days as the flavours will
then blend together. Will keep up to 2 further days in the
fridge.

Serve refrigerator relish with spicy potatoes, cold left-
overs and in fresh bread rolls with nut pâté.

11

CAKES, DESSERTS
AND TOPPINGS

GENERAL INFORMATION
ON CAKES

* Cold-pressed oils and butter provide the fat in our recipes.

* Our cakes provide healthy sources of carbohydrates but they should be eaten, like everything else, in moderation!

* Test to check whether a cake is cooked by inserting a thin knife, a toothpick or a cake-testing needle in the centre and if it comes out clean then the cake is done. The edges of the cake will also begin to shrink from the sides of the tin.

NOTES ON COMMON INGREDIENTS

The *baking powder* we use in our cake recipes is very easy to prepare and keeps well in a screw-top jar:

> equal quantities of cream of tartar, arrowroot and potassium bicarbonate

There is a salt-free baking powder now available in health stores which also includes potato flour in place of arrowroot. It is very expensive though.

The *fruit purées* referred to in the recipes are simply made from blended or liquidised stewed dried fruits and their syrup. We usually make a large amount, refrigerate some and freeze the rest:

Stew approx. 2 lb (1 kilo) dried fruit, for example dates or Hunza apricots, in a saucepan without a lid with approx 2 pt, (1 litre) water.

Fruit syrup – Stewed Hunza apricots in their stewing juice produce a thick syrup after standing in the fridge for 24 hours. This syrup is an economical substitute for malt or fruit juice concentrates. The apricots, stoned and processed, make a delicious spread or dessert topping.

Vanilla extract is made from a vanilla pod. Put a vanilla pod in a saucepan with 4 fl oz (110ml, ½ cup) water. Bring to the boil, lower the heat and simmer for 10 minutes. Turn off the heat and cool. Remove the vanilla pod, dry and store in a screw-top jar. It may be re-used until it loses its flavour. Store the extract in another jar in the fridge.

Basic Sponge Cake (1)
Fills two 10" (25cm) sandwich cake tins
Preparation time 45 mins.

   ghee
   4 oz (110g, ½ cup) butter, soft
   3 tbsp malt
   2 egg yolks
   1 tbsp vanilla extract (see above)
   6 oz (170g, 1½ cups) brown rice flour (organic)
   6 oz (170g, 1 cup) wholewheat flour (organic)
   1 rounded tbsp baking powder (see opposite)
   8 fl oz (225ml, 1 cup) pineapple juice
   2 egg whites

Preheat the oven at gas 4 (180°C, 350°F). Grease two 10″ (25cm) sandwich cake tins with ghee. Cream the butter and malt together, beat in the egg yolks and vanilla. Combine all the dry ingredients in another bowl. Add this dry mixture to the wet mixture a little at a time, also pouring in the pineapple juice. Beat this batter vigorously. Whisk the egg whites until they form soft peaks. Fold them into the cake batter. Pour into the prepared tins and bake for 25-30 minutes. Turn onto a wire tray to cool. Store in an airtight container in a cool place, or freeze.

Basic Sponge (2)
Preparation time 30 mins.   *Fills one 10″ (25cm) cake tin*

  ghee
6 tbsp cold-pressed grapeseed or sunflower oil
3 tbsp concentrated sweetener (2 tbsp apple juice
    concentrate and 1 tbsp malt or other combination)
2 eggs free-range and organic
1 tbsp home-made vanilla extract (p. 147)
6 oz (170g) wholewheat flour, organic
2 tsp baking powder (p. 146)

Preheat the oven at gas 4 (180°C, 350°F). Grease one round 10″ (25cm) cake tin with ghee. Combine all the wet ingredients in a mixing bowl or processor and beat vigorously. Sift the flour and baking powder together and mix into the wet mixture gradually. Pour into the prepared cake tin and bake for 20 minutes. Turn out onto a wire rack to cool. Store in an airtight container in a cool place or freeze.

Variations: (1) substitute coconut, soya flour, carob flour or wheatgerm for 2 oz (55g) of the flour, or (2) fold in 4 oz (110g, ⅔ cup) sultanas or any other dried or fresh fruit after the final whisking of the batter. The addition of 4 oz (110g) grated carrot and 1 tsp allspice makes another delicious variation. (3) For an eggless version simply increase the amount of baking powder to 1 rounded tablespoonful.

* You can adapt the same recipe to make carob brownies.

Use 3 tbsp malt and 2 oz (55g) wholewheat flour, 2 oz (55g) carob flour and 2 oz (55g) soya flour in place of the 6 oz (170g) wholewheat flour. Add 4 oz (110g, 1 cup) chopped walnuts before pouring into the cake tin and baking.

Fruit Cake

Preparation time 1¼ hours   Fills an 8" (20cm) cake tin

ghee
1 lb (450g, 3 cups) mixed dried fruit (unsulphured)
5 fl oz (150ml, ⅔ cup) water or fresh fruit juice
8 oz (225g, 1⅓ cups) wholewheat flour, organic
1 tsp powdered cinnamon
1 tsp powdered mixed spice
1 tsp baking powder (p. 146)
grated rind of 1 orange (only if unsprayed or organic)
3 tbsp cold pressed sunflower oil
2 eggs, beaten free-range and organic

Grease an 8" (20cm) round fruit cake tin or a 2 lb (900g) loaf tin with ghee. Line it with greaseproof or brown paper. Wash the dried fruit and add the water or juice. Bring to the boil and simmer for 5 minutes. Remove from the heat and allow to cool. Sieve all the dry ingredients together into a bowl.

Preheat the oven at gas 4 (180°C, 350°F). When the fruit has cooled, add the orange rind, oil and beaten eggs to it. Stir in the dry ingredients and mix well. Pour the mixture into the prepared cake tin and bake in the centre of the oven for about an hour. Cool in the tin. Store well-wrapped in greaseproof paper and in an airtight container or freeze.

* We adapt this recipe for our *Christmas cake*. We make it at the end of October and treble the amounts to fill a 10" (25cm) deep fruit cake tin. We always include chopped unsulphured whole apricots in the fruit, substitute 4 oz (110g, ⅔ cup) of the flour with the same amount of ground almonds and add a little pure neat whisky at intervals between baking and serving! (When adding alcohol to a cake simply turn it upside down, prick the base with a kitchen fork and pour 2 tbsp evenly over the surface.)

Another favourite variation is to make the basic recipe with either all dates or all figs instead of mixed fruit.

Fudge Cake (without eggs)
Preparation time 1 hour   *Fills a 10" (25cm) cake tin*

4 fl oz (110ml, ½ cup) cold-pressed sunflower oil
6 fl oz (170ml, ¾ cup) malt
1 tbsp vanilla extract (p. 147)
6 fl oz (170ml, ¾ cup) diluted apple concentrate
   (1 part juice to 8 parts water)
2½ oz (75g, ¾ cup) carob flour
12 oz (340g, 4½ cups) soya flour or a mixture of 2 parts
   soya flour to 1 part brown rice flour, organic
1 tbsp baking powder (p. 146)

Preheat the oven at gas 4 (180°C, 350°F). Grease a 10" (25cm) round cake tin. Using a mixer or processor combine all the wet ingredients and beat vigorously. Add the dry ingredients and mix well. Transfer the mixture into the prepared cake tin and bake for about 40 minutes. Cool in the tin for a few minutes and then on a wire tray. Store in an airtight container in the fridge or freezer.

* This cake becomes even stickier after a day or two!

Gingerbread
Preparation time 1¼ hours   *Makes 10–12 squares*

2 eggs, free-range and organic preferably
4 tbsp of each: molasses, malt, cold-pressed oil, hot
   water
8 oz (225g, 1⅓ cups) wholewheat flour, organic
1 tsp baking powder (p. 146)
½ tsp dried ginger
1 tsp grated fresh root ginger
½ tsp powdered cinnamon
¼ tsp grated nutmeg
2 oz (55g, ½ cup) sultanas, floured

Preheat the oven at gas 4 (180°C, 350°F). Grease a baking tray, 12″ × 8″ × 1½″ (30cm × 20cm × 4cm). Combine all the wet ingredients together and beat vigorously. In a separate bowl combine all the dry ingredients except the sultanas. Add the dry ingredients to the wet and beat again. Fold in the sultanas. Pour the mixture into the prepared tray and bake for 45 minutes – 1 hour. Cool slightly before cutting. Keep the gingerbread in the tray until cold. Store in an airtight container or freeze.

STEAMED PUDDINGS

Use the Basic Sponge cake mixture (2) (p. 148) including wheatgerm with the flour when steaming a sponge pudding.

Sweet Syrupy Pudding
Preparation time 1¼ hours   (serves 6)

    ghee
    juice and rind, if unsprayed, of 1 lemon
    1 lb (450g, 3½ cups) dried Hunza apricots,
        soaked and stewed for 15 minutes
    basic sponge mixture

Grease a 1 lb (450g) pudding basin. Mix the lemon juice and grated rind with the stewed apricots, and transfer them into the basin. Pour sufficient water into a saucepan (with a lid and which is large enough to hold the basin) to reach a third of the way up the sides of the pan. Bring to the boil while you make up the basic sponge mixture. Spoon this on top of the apricots. Cover the basin with a double layer of greaseproof paper secured with string and stand it on a vegetable steamer or in a small metal colander in the water in the saucepan. Put a lid on your saucepan and let the water go on boiling gently for about an hour. (Watch the water level – it may need topping up.)

Plum Pudding

(makes 2 × 2 lb (900g) puddings)
Preparation time 4½ hours and overnight

8 oz (225g, 1⅓ cups) of each: raisins, currants, sultanas
4 oz (110g, ⅔ cup) wholewheat flour, organic
8 oz (225g, 2 cups) wholewheat breadcrumbs, organic
4 oz (110g, 1 cup) candied peel (p. 182)
1 tbsp ground almonds
juice and rind of 1 lemon (rind only if unsprayed)
½ tsp of each: cinnamon, mixed spice
1 tsp grated fresh ginger
5 tbsp cold-pressed sunflower oil
10 fl oz (300ml, 1¼ cups) brown ale
ghee

Wash and drain the fruit. Combine all the ingredients
together in a bowl, mix well, cover and leave to stand
overnight. Grease two 2 lb (900g) basins with ghee and fill
with the pudding mixture. Cover each basin with a double
layer of greaseproof paper, secured with string. Sit the basins
on steamers in saucepans, pour in sufficient boiling water to
reach halfway up the sides of the basins. Put the lids on.
Steam for 4 hours. Top up with more boiling water if
required.

* When cooked, take out of the basins and serve or wrap in
fresh greaseproof paper and store in a cool place. Plum
puddings usually keep well but keep an eye on yours.
Sometimes, if there is too much moisture inside the
wrapping paper, mould grows. Store in the fridge or freezer.
Steam for 2 hours before serving.

* Home-made mincemeat can easily be made and stored
refrigerated for about 6 weeks. Simply finely chop washed
dried fruit (currants, raisins and sultanas), sharp eating
apples and almonds in the ratio 6:2:1 respectively and mix
with one orange to each half pound of apples used, a little
mixed spice and nutmeg to taste. A little brandy is a delicious
optional addition!

DESSERTS

Non-Dairy Ice Cream
Preparation time 1½ hours   *(serves 6)*

    8 oz (225g) tofu
    5 fl oz (150ml, ⅔ cup) soya milk
    2 ripe bananas
    2 tsp raw honey
    6 tbsp fruit juice – pineapple, apple
    3 tsp agar-agar powder dissolved in a little water
    a little pure vanilla, almond oil or other pure, natural
      flavouring

Blend all the ingredients together until creamy. Pour into a
freezer container, freeze for about 30 minutes, take out and
whisk. Return to the freezer. Repeat this whisking twice
more to prevent ice crystals forming and then serve as a
creamy topping or leave in the freezer until completely
frozen.

FRUIT SPECIALS

Orange and Strawberry Salad
                                    (serves 6)
Preparation time 10 mins. and refrigerate for 1 hour

    8 oz (225g) strawberries
    6 oranges
    rind of 2 oranges (only if unsprayed)
    freshly squeezed orange juice
    mint

Wash the strawberries (p. 33). Drain and place them in a
serving bowl. Grate the orange rind over the strawberries.
Remove the pith from the oranges and then slice them.
Arrange them on top of the strawberries. Add a little orange
juice and decorate the salad with sprigs of mint. Cover and
refrigerate for an hour before serving.

Sam's Fried Dates and Bananas

A simple yet delicious dessert which we serve with chilled banana ice-cream (p. 155)

Preparation time 10 mins.   *(serves 2-3)*

   a handful of dates
   ghee
   1 banana
   1 tsp desiccated coconut

Wash and dry the dates. Stone if desired. Heat a heavy pan and grease it lightly with ghee. Fry the dates, put them on a plate and keep hot. Peel the banana, slice it lengthwise and fry. Place the strips of fried banana on top of the dates. Lightly toast the coconut under the grill and sprinkle on top of the fruit. Serve immediately while hot with banana ice-cream.

Oven-baked Pineapple

Preparation time 15 mins.   *(serves 4)*

   1 pineapple
   ghee

Peel and cut a pineapple into quarters from the top and lay each one on a lightly greased tray. Bake for about 10 minutes at gas 4 (180°C, 350°F). Delicious served with hot custard or a fruit sauce.

Barbecued Fruit

Choose firm but ripe fruit – pineapple, peaches, ápricots. Wash the fruit thoroughly (p. 33). Cut into chunks and skewer. Hold over barbecue coals for a few minutes. Serve immediately with a selection of sauces or dips.

Fruit Fluffs

Blenders and food processors are the answer to a busy cook's prayer! Light, fresh nutritious desserts can be whisked up in seconds.

Combinations of raw, cooked and dried fruits and vegetables with the addition of a little spice, lemon juice and occasionally a little honey produce instant foamy desserts, toppings and pie and flan fillings.

Soft fruits both local and from abroad are ideal.

Apple and Apricot Fluff
Preparation time overnight, and 30 mins.   *(serves 4–6)*

24 dried whole apricots, unsulphured
6 sharp eating apples, unsprayed
½ tsp powdered cinnamon
apple juice
2 small, ripe bananas

Wash the apricots, cover with water and leave to soak overnight. Wash and peel the apples and slice them into a saucepan. Add the cinnamon and just enough juice to cover the bottom of the pan, bring to the boil and simmer until soft. Cool. Blend all the ingredients together until light and fluffy. Serve immediately.

Frozen Bananas
Never be without these in the freezer! Simply peel bananas and freeze. When frozen bananas are processed, using the sharp metal blade in a processor, they magically become creamy in texture and can be used as ice-cream. When frozen on sticks without their skins they become delicious lollies. Alternatively dip firm but ripe bananas in malt or date purée, roll in coconut or ground-nuts, and freeze.

Peach Cream
Preparation time 5 mins.   *(serves 4–6)*

2 large, frozen, ripe bananas
4 frozen ripe peaches
1 tbsp cashew pieces
up to a cupful of pineapple juice

Process all the ingredients together until thick and creamy and serve.

Other Combinations

To the above recipe omitting the peaches add any of the following:

1. frozen soft fruits – blackcurrants, strawberries, raspberries;
2. peanut butter;
3. chopped walnuts and maple syrup;
4. carob powder and a few drops of pure peppermint oil;
5. chopped pecans and raisins (untreated).

Tangy Banana Cream
Preparation time 5 mins.   *(serves 2–3)*

    8 oz (225g) tofu, soft preferably (p. 185)
    2 ripe bananas
    2 tsp frozen grapefruit concentrate
    2 tsp vanilla extract (p. 147)
    1 tsp raw honey
    garnish – mint and grapes

Blend all the ingredients together except the garnish. Pour into dessert glasses, decorate with mint and a few grapes and chill. Keeps up to 2 days in the fridge.

PIES AND TARTS

Pineapple Tart
Preparation time 1¼ hours   *(serves 6)*

Pastry Case

    ghee
    1 tbsp wholewheat flour, organic
    2 tbsp wheatgerm
    2 tbsp oats (organic)

2 tbsp unsweetened, desiccated coconut
2 tbsp chopped walnuts
4 tbsp cold-pressed sunflower oil
3 tbsp malt

Preheat the oven at gas 5 (190°C, 375°F). Grease one 10″ (25cm) pie plate. Combine all the dry ingredients in a bowl and then mix in the oil. Add the malt and stir well. Press the mixture into the prepared pie plate and bake for 10–15 minutes. Cool.

Filling

8 oz (225g) quark or soft goat cheese
2 tbsp home-made candied peel (p. 182)
2 tbsp chopped pineapple
2–3 slices of pineapple

Mix the cheese, candied peel and pineapple together lightly. Spoon into the baked pie crust and chill in the fridge for at least an hour before serving. Will keep for up to 24 hours in the fridge and may be frozen.

Pumpkin Pie
Preparation time 1½ hours   *(serves 6)*

ghee
8 oz chilled oil-based pastry (p. 70)
8 fl oz (225ml, 1 cup) water
1 tbsp soya flour
2 eggs, free-range and organic
1 tbsp apple concentrate
1 tbsp malt or concentrated apple juice
1 tbsp vanilla extract (p. 147)
1 tbsp molasses
1 tsp powdered cinnamon
½ tsp grated nutmeg
½ tsp grated fresh root ginger
12 oz (340g, 1½ cups) mashed cooked pumpkin (peeled, seeded and gently stewed until soft in just enough water to cover the base of the pan)

Preheat the oven at gas 5 (190°C, 375°F). Grease a 10″ (25cm) pie plate with ghee. Roll out the pastry and line the plate. Blend all the filling ingredients together and pour into the pastry case. Bake for 15 minutes and then lower the temperature to gas 4 (180°C, 350°F) and bake for a further 30–40 minutes or until firm at the centre. Will keep for 24 hours in the fridge and can be frozen.

Almond Tart
Preparation time 1 hour (serves 4–6)

Tart Crust

  ghee
  8 oz (225g, 1⅓ cups) wholewheat flour, organic
  4 oz (110g) butter or 4 tbsp cold-pressed sesame oil
  2 egg yolks free-range, organic
  3–6 tbsp chilled orange juice

Grease a 10″ (25cm) pie dish with ghee. Measure the flour into a mixing bowl. Cut the butter into small cubes and rub the butter into the flour until the mixture resembles fine breadcrumbs. Or using a metal knife or fork, combine the flour and oil. Stir in the egg yolks. Gradually add sufficient orange juice to form a ball of dough. Cover the bowl and chill the dough in the fridge for 30 minutes. Roll out and line the greased pie dish.

Filling

  4–6 tbsp sugar-free raspberry spread
  2 egg whites
  1 tbsp maple syrup
  ½ tsp pure vanilla essence
  ½ tsp pure almond oil
  1 tbsp finely chopped almonds

Preheat the oven at gas 6 (200°C, 400°F) if you have used butter in the pastry; otherwise gas 5 (190°C, 375°F). Spread the raspberry jam evenly over the pastry base. Whisk the egg

whites until peaks can be raised. Continue to beat as you
gradually add the maple syrup. When the beaten whites form
stiff peaks fold in the vanilla essence, almond oil and ground
almonds. Pile this meringue mixture quickly over the pastry
base and bake for 25–30 minutes.

Blackcurrant Cheesecake
Preparation time 1¼ hours plus 2 hours in fridge

(serves 6)

Base

> 2 tbsp malt
> 6oz (170g, 2 cups) oats
> 6 oz (170g, 1½ cups) crushed walnuts

Measure the malt into a saucepan using an oiled spoon and
warm slightly to thin it. Combine the oats and the crushed
walnuts with the malt. Press over the base of a 10″ (25cm) pie
dish and chill well.

Filling

> 1¼ lb (570g) soft or firm tofu (p. 185)
> 4 fl oz (110ml, ½ cup) lemon juice
> juice and grated rind of 1 lemon (only use the rind if
>   unsprayed)
> 1 tbsp vanilla extract (p. 147)
> 5 tbsp fruit juice concentrate
> 2 tbsp cold-pressed sunflower oil
> 2 tbsp brown rice flour, organic

Preheat the oven at gas 4 (180°C, 350°F). Combine all the
filling ingredients together and blend to a smooth cream.
Spoon evenly onto the base. Bake for about 35 minutes or
until firm. Cool.

Top with blackcurrant topping:

> 6 oz (170g, 1½ cups) fresh blackcurrants
> apple juice

Blackcurrant Cheesecake—contd.
2-3 sprigs sweet cicely, if available
4 tbsp concentrated apple and blackcurrant juice
juice and grated rind of a lemon (only use the rind if unsprayed or organic)
1 tbsp arrowroot mixed to a paste with 1 tbsp water

Wash the blackcurrants (p. 33). Put them in a saucepan with just sufficient apple juice to cover the bottom of the pan; add the sweet cicely, concentrated juice and the juice and grated rind of the lemon. Mix the arrowroot paste and add to the stewing fruit, stirring continuously for about 10 minutes until this topping thickens. Spread evenly over the cooled cheesecake and refrigerate for at least 2 hours.

Apricot Slices
Preparation time 40 mins. and overnight   (serves 8-10)

8 oz (225g) Hunza apricots
8 oz (225g) apricot pieces (unsulphured)
ghee
5 fl oz (150ml, ⅔ cup) cold-pressed sunflower oil
2 tbsp malt
2-3 tbsp apple concentrate
8 oz (225g, 2⅔ cups) oats, organic
8 oz (225g, 1⅓ cups) wholewheat flour, organic
1 tsp powdered cinnamon

Wash and soak all the apricots overnight. Next day, preheat the oven at gas 5 (190°C, 375°F). Grease a baking pan 12″×8″ (30cm × 20cm) with ghee. Remove the stones from the Hunza apricots and purée all of the apricots. Put aside.

Combine the oil and malt in a food mixer or processor or warm them slightly, stirring them together in a saucepan. Add the apple concentrate to this malted oil. In a larger separate mixing bowl combine the dry ingredients. Now stir in the malt, oil and apple mixture to make a tacky oat mixture. Spread three-quarters of this evenly over the bottom of the baking tin. Spread the apricot purée on the oat base and then fork over the remaining oat mixture as evenly as possible on top of the apricot purée. Bake for about 30 minutes. Cut into slices.

Apple Peasant
Preparation time 25 mins. and overnight   *(serves 6)*

   2½ lb (1.1kg) cooking apples
   3–4 sprigs sweet cicely
   5 tbsp apple juice concentrate
   a little water
   8 oz (225g, 1⅓ cups) figs (chopped) or sultanas
   2 tbsp cold-pressed sunflower oil
   3 tbsp malt
   1 lb (450g, 5 cups) oats, organic
   4 oz (110g, ½ cup) sesame seeds

Wash, slice and stew the apples with the sweet cicely, apple concentrate and a little water. Remove from the heat when soft. Take out the herb. Cool the apple mixture and purée it. Wash, drain and chop the figs and stir them into the apple purée. Warm the oil and malt together until thin (it is easier to measure the oil first and then use the oiled spoon to measure the malt). Combine the oats, sesame seeds, and the oil and malt mixture. Mix well. Ladle a little apple purée into an 8″ (20cm) deep glass dessert bowl, spread a layer of the oat mixture on top, add another layer of apple purée and top again with the oat mixture. Continue to alternate layers until all the fruit and oat mixtures are used. Chill overnight. Spread a layer of cashew cream (p. 164) on the top and sprinkle with desiccated coconut or grated carob.

FRUIT CRUMBLES

Varied fruit mixtures in crumbles make them a favourite family pudding. Simply grease a pudding basin, put in chopped fresh fruit and/or dried fruit (this may be stewed first), sufficient boiling water or fruit juice to cover the bottom of the basin and then top it all with a crumble topping. Bake at gas 5 (190°C, 375°F) for about 30 minutes.

Try:

..... apples, sultanas, and cinnamon;
..... Hunza apricots and gooseberries;
..... gooseberries with elderflowers;
..... figs and bananas;
..... rhubarb and cinnamon.

Try different toppings by lightly mixing 1 part butter or oil to 3 parts flour or similar:

..... wholewheat flour, sesame seeds and butter or oil;
..... brown rice flour, butter and unsweetened desiccated coconut;
..... wholewheat flour, oatmeal, cinnamon, oil;
..... granola;
..... wholewheat flour, okara (ground, cooked soya beans) and unsweetened desiccated coconut.

COLD SUMMER TREATS

Sweet Rice Mould
Preparation time 20 mins. and overnight   *(serves 6)*

> ghee
> 2 bananas, sliced
> lemon juice
> 1½ lb (675g, 4 cups) cooked, cold brown rice
> 4 tbsp home-made candied peel (p. 182)
> 1 tbsp pumpkin seeds
> 2 oz (55g) grapes, diced

Grease a 2 lb (900g) pudding basin or a ring mould. Peel and slice the bananas into rounds and toss them in the lemon juice. Combine all the ingredients together so that they are distributed evenly in the mixture and press this firmly into the basin. Cover with a plate and refrigerate overnight. Turn out of the basin before serving, and decorate with home-made yoghurt and fresh fruit of your choice.

Summer Pudding
Preparation time 20 mins. and overnight   (serves 4)

1 lb (450g, 4 cups) soft fruit – raspberries,
    strawberries, blackberries, currants
2 tbsp pure apple juice or apple juice concentrate
ghee
slices of wholewheat bread, organic

Wash the fruit (p. 33). Drain well. Stew the fruit gently in the
apple juice for about 10 minutes. Grease a pudding basin
with ghee while the fruit cools and line it with slices of
wholewheat bread, crusts as well! Spoon in some of the fruit
mixture, cover with a layer of bread and continue to
alternate layers of fruit and bread. Cover with a plate and
some heavy object and refrigerate in your fridge overnight.
Turn out of the basin to serve. Freezes successfully.

* The addition of some uncooked fruit to the cooked gives
this dessert an interesting texture.

TOPPINGS, SAUCES AND FILLINGS
FOR CAKES AND DESSERTS

The simplest toppings are often the most pleasing. Our
favourites are toasted or raw chopped nuts and seeds – hazel
nuts, almonds, coconut, sunflower seeds, poppy and sesame
seeds. Many of the "icing" type toppings and fillings which
follow include such simple favourites too.

Almond Paste
Preparation time 15 mins.

8 oz (225g, 2 cups) almonds
2 eggs, free-range and organic
2 rounded tbsp malt
2–4 drops pure almond oil
4 heaped tbsp soya flour
4 heaped tbsp brown rice flour

Grind the almonds. Beat the eggs with the malt and almond oil in a food mixer, blender or processor. Transfer this mixture to a larger bowl and stir in the ground almonds. Add the flours 1 tablespoon at a time, alternating between the soya and the brown rice flour at each addition. Add sufficient to bind the mixture into a stiff dough. Can be frozen until required. Otherwise knead lightly, roll out on a floured board and transfer to the top of your cake.

As well as for topping cakes, use this almond paste to fill prunes and apricots for party treats. Simply cut an opening down one side, remove any stones and fill with a little almond paste. Sandwich walnut halves together too.

* A little orange flower water added to the almond paste mixture results in a different delicate flavour for a filling.

Cashew Cream
Preparation time overnight and 5 mins.

   1 cup cashews
   1 cup water or apple juice

Soak the cashews overnight and blend together.

Creamy Yoghurt Topping
Preparation time 10 mins.

   8 oz (225g, 1 cup) soft tofu or quark (p. 185)
   1 tbsp natural yoghurt
   1 tsp pure vanilla essence and/or 1 tsp lemon juice
   1–2 tbsp raw honey

Whisk the tofu or quark until it becomes fluffy. Stir in the yoghurt and vanilla. Beat this mixture and continue to beat while you slowly trickle in the honey. The topping mixture will thicken.

Carob Topping
Preparation time 35 mins.

   5 tbsp carob flour
   12 fl oz (350ml, 1½ cups) water
   1 tsp vanilla essence or 1 tbsp home-made extract (p. 147)
   2 tbsp soya flour
   2 oz (55g, ⅓ cup) raisins or other dried fruit
   2 tsp arrowroot mixed to a paste with 2 tsp water
   2 tbsp tahini

Bring the carob flour and water to the boil and then simmer for 10 minutes. Add the vanilla, soya flour and raisins and continue to cook for a further 10–15 minutes. Add the arrowroot paste and stir until thick. Blend the mixture in a blender or processor and lastly stir in the tahini to make an even thicker topping.

Orange Carob Frosting
Preparation time 5 mins.

   2 fl oz (50ml, ⅓ cup) light tahini
   2 fl oz (50ml, ⅓ cup) orange juice concentrate
   1 tbsp carob powder

Combine all the ingredients together and spread as a cake frosting.

Nut and Carob Topping
Preparation time 5 mins.

   1 tbsp peanut butter (salt- and sugar-free)
   1 tbsp carob powder
   water

Blend the peanut butter and carob powder together. Add a little water to make a spreading consistency.

Coconut Topping
Preparation time 10 mins.

2 tbsp brown rice flour
4 fl oz (110g, ½ cup) water
2 tsp butter
2 tsp raw honey
4 tsp unsweetened desiccated coconut

Combine the rice flour with the water, bring to the boil, then lower the heat and simmer until thick, stirring all the time. Blend with the butter and the honey. Add the coconut.

Butter Nut Glaze
Preparation time 5 mins.

2 tbsp ghee
1 tbsp malt
1 tbsp chopped nuts

Mix the ghee and malt together and then add the chopped nuts.

SUGAR-FREE SPREADS

Apricot Spread
Preparation time 25 mins.

1 lb (450g) dried, unsulphured apricots
apple or pineapple juice
1-2 tsp

1-2 tsp cinnamon

Wash the apricots, put them in a saucepan, add enough fruit juice or water to cover them and cook until they are soft and there is very little liquid left. Cool. Blend with the cinnamon. Store in a screw-top jar in the fridge. Freezes well.

Apple Spread
Preparation time 3½ hours

> 5 lb (2½ kilos) sharp eating apples
> apple or white grape juice
> 2 tsp lemon juice
> 1 tsp of each – cinnamon, nutmeg, cloves

Wash and slice the apples (only peel them first if they have been sprayed). Put them in a saucepan and cover with apple or grape juice and lemon juice. Bring to the boil and then simmer until soft. Remove from the heat and blend in a liquidiser or processor. Add the spices and return to the heat. Bring back to the boil and then simmer for 2–3 hours, stirring from time to time, until the mixture is thick. Store in screw-top jars or freeze in freezer containers.

Soft Fruit Spreads

Our harvest of soft fruits is large enough to enable us to freeze plenty. Bagged in 2 lb (1 kilo) amounts (the most convenient quantity for our family), we can have an almost continuous supply of fruit through the winter, which is a great saving.

* Open freezing is especially successful. Simply lay the fruits on trays, freeze uncovered and then bag when frozen. Strawberries benefit from being sliced in half before open freezing.

> lecithin
> 2 lb (900g) soft fruit, fresh or frozen
> 2 pt (1.1 litres, 5 cups) fruit juice (apple or grape)
>   including any juice from the fruit
> 1 tbsp agar-agar flakes

Put the soft fruit into a saucepan which has been brushed with lecithin. Heat and allow the fruit to soften. When the juice from the fruit begins to appear, strain this into a measuring jug and add grape or apple juice to make up the full measure.

Pour this liquid over the fruit, sprinkle the agar-agar

flakes on the surface and stir gently. Bring to the boil and simmer for 5 minutes until the agar-agar flakes have dissolved. Cool, pour into screw-top jars and refrigerate. Keeps about a week in the fridge.

* Alternatively, stew the fruit very lightly with 2 or 3 sprigs of sweet cicely. This will sweeten the fruit slightly. Cool, remove the herbs, purée and then stir in some honey to taste. Keep in a covered container in the fridge – it will last for about a week.

* Dried fruits, washed, chopped and soaked overnight also make delicious spreads. Wash, stew gently for about 15 minutes and purée.

FRUITY AND CREAMY ICE TOPPINGS

There are a few recipes in the dessert section which also make delicious toppings, particularly the Fruit Fluffs on p. 154. Here are a few more suggestions which can be used as partially frozen or frozen toppings:

..... Partially freeze fruit juices in ice trays for 20 minutes, whisk and refreeze. Whisk again 2 or 3 times in the following half hour and use or allow to freeze hard.
..... Partially freeze a mixture of goat milk and fruit juice and continue as above.
..... Partially freeze a mixture of goat milk, a little honey and vanilla. Whisk and refreeze 3 times within 40 minutes.
..... Partially freeze soya milk blended with raspberries and a little honey and continue as above.

Tropical Fruit Sauce

(makes about 1 pt, 550ml, 2½ cups)
Preparation time 15 mins.

1 ripe papaya, skinned
1 ripe mango, skinned
1 pt (550ml, 2½ cups) orange and passion fruit juice
pinch of cinnamon and allspice
2 tsp arrowroot mixed to a paste with 2 tsp water

Wash all the fruit (p. 33). Blend the fruit with the orange and passion fruit juice and spices. Put the mixture into a saucepan and bring to the boil. Remove from the heat and add the arrowroot paste. Mix well. Return to the heat, bring back to the boil and cook, stirring continuously, for 5 minutes or until the sauce thickens.

Stewed fruits can be easily turned into sauces if thickened with arrowroot (p. 184):

..... Gooseberries stewed with 1–2 sprays of elderflowers in apple juice, then blended (without the herb), thickened with arrowroot and chilled. This can be sweetened with raw honey when cool.
..... Rhubarb, apple and freshly grated ginger – stewed, blended, set with agar-agar, chilled slightly before sweetening with raw honey and allowed to set in the fridge.
..... Apples and dried apricots stewed as in the apple and apricot spreads recipes (p. 166), plus chopped walnuts.
..... Stew a mixture of fresh blackcurrants and dried currants with a little lemon juice.
..... Stew diced pears with cranberries, cool and add raw honey to sweeten.
..... Poach strawberries with 1 or 2 sliced oranges.

Fudge Sauce

Preparation time 10-15 mins.   *(fills a small cream jug)*

1 tbsp ghee
1 tbsp malt or fruit juice concentrate
1 tbsp carob flour
1 tbsp brown rice flour
2 tbsp soya flour
8 fl oz (225ml, 1 cup) water

Measure the ghee and the malt into a saucepan and warm them until they become thinner. Add the flours and the water and mix well. Bring to the boil, stirring continuously. Simmer for 5-10 minutes, or until thick and fudgy.

Custard Sauce

Preparation time 20 mins.   *(makes 1 pt, 550ml, 2½ cups)*

1 vanilla pod
1 pt (550ml, 2½ cups) goat or soya milk
2 egg yolks, free-range and organic
1 tbsp arrowroot mixed to a paste with 1 tbsp of milk
   (optional)

Put the vanilla pod in the milk in a double boiler (a pyrex bowl sitting firmly over a saucepan of boiling water works just as well) and warm. Beat the egg yolks and add them to the milk. Stir well. If you wish to make a thick custard add the arrowroot paste at this point. Continue to stir until the custard thickens. Lastly remove the vanilla pod.

12

DRINKS WITH A DIFFERENCE

HERB TEAS

All my family enjoy herb teas. The younger members prefer raspberry leaf, lemon verbena, mint, and mint and chamomile whilst the others like chamomile on its own, lime blossom, elderflower and sage. We buy the loose, dried herbs in preference to sachets because they're cheaper!

Make herb tea by infusing 1 heaped tbsp of dried herbs in 2 pt (1 litre, 4 cups) of boiling water. Steep for 5 minutes. (A rough estimate is 1 tsp of dried herb per person.)

If you have fresh herbs in your garden try infusing a few sprigs or a handful of them. Fresh sage and fresh lemon balm are among our favourites.

Chilled herb teas (mint, spearmint, lemon verbena, lemon balm and rosehip) are particularly enjoyable. They are also delicious as a punch base to mix with your choice of fruit juice and serve with slices of fresh orange and ice.

Mixed Fruit Punch
(makes approx. 3½ pt, 1½ litres, 8 cups)
Preparation time 15 mins.

    1 cup orange juice
    1 cup pineapple juice
    1 cup apple juice
    1 cup chilled lemon balm, lemon verbena or mint tea
    2 cups naturally sparkling mineral water
    lemon balm, lemon verbena or mint leaves
    slices of orange
    ice cubes

Combine the juices, chilled tea and mineral water in a jug.
Add a few leaves of the herb used and a few thin slices of
fresh orange as decoration. Add ice to keep cool if required.

Mulled Apple Punch
(makes approx. 2 pt, 1 litre, 4 cups)
Preparation time 1 hour

   4 cups apple juice made by diluting apple concentrate,
      1 part juice to 8 parts water
   2 sliced lemons
   2 sliced oranges
   1 stick of cinnamon
   1 cup raisins, untreated and washed

Place all the ingredients in a saucepan, cover and heat gently
for about an hour. Serve hot.

SMOOTHIES

We learned to make smoothies in America when we acquired
our processor having never owned even a blender before!
The latter does the job as well.
   Accurate measuring of ingredients isn't too important in
the following recipes. The quantities are per person and any
cup will do but use the same one throughout a recipe for
multiple quantities.

Banana Smoothie
(per person)

   1 banana
   1 cup cold goat or soya milk
   ½ tsp vanilla essence
   ½ tsp blackstrap molasses

Whisk or blend in a food processor or liquidiser all the ingredients. Drink immediately.

More Smoothies
These have a milk base like the banana one but you can ring the changes on the milk and other ingredients. An alternative base, to make more of a snack than a drink, is to put in yoghurt instead of milk. For home-made yoghurt see p. 36.

To 1 cup of milk (goat, soya, nut or seed) add any of the following and whisk or blend in a food processor or blender:

..... 1 banana, 3 tbsp goat or soya yoghurt, 1–2 tbsp peanut butter.

..... 1 banana, 3 tbsp goat or soya yoghurt, 3 lightly steamed carrots.

..... 1 tsp carob powder (mixed to a paste with a little milk), 1 tsp molasses, 1 tbsp unsweetened desiccated coconut.

..... 1 cup chopped melon, sprinkling of ginger.

..... 1 cup orange juice, 1–2 tsp raw honey.

..... 1 tbsp date or apricot purée.

..... 1 cup unsweetened desiccated coconut, 1–2 drops of pure almond oil.

..... 1 cup apple juice, sprinkling of cinnamon.

..... ½ cup of hulled soft fruit (raspberries, strawberries, blackcurrants), a little raw honey.

..... ½ cup stoned chopped fresh apricots and/or peaches, 1–2 drops pure vanilla or almond oil.

..... ¼ cup yoghurt, ¼ cup orange juice, ½ cup pineapple juice.

..... 1 tbsp chopped fresh pineapple, 1 tbsp freshly grated coconut.

..... 1 cup orange juice, 2 frozen bananas.

..... 2 tbsp peanut butter, 1 frozen banana, 1 tsp pure vanilla essence, a little raw honey (optional), cubes of frozen goat milk.

FRUIT JUICE SHAKES

Strawberry Shake

(makes approx. 1 pt, 500ml, 2 cups)

1 cup hulled strawberries
1 ripe banana
2 cups apple juice, chilled

Blend all the ingredients together.

Other combinations (per 2 shakes)

..... 2 cups pineapple juice, 1 banana, 2–4 tbsp apricot
purée.

..... 1 cup apple juice, 1 banana, 2 tsp carob powder (mixed
to a paste first with a little juice).

..... 1 cup apple juice, 1 cup chopped fresh pineapple, 1 tsp
unsweetened, desiccated coconut, 1 tbsp ground
almonds or sunflower seeds, crushed ice cubes.

..... 1½ tsp freshly grated ginger, 2–2½ cups of apple and
cherry juice, crushed ice cubes.

UNUSUAL JUICES

If you own an electric juicer you have a wide variety of
combinations of vegetables and fruits available with which
to experiment. Here are some pleasing mixtures:

..... beetroot and carrots
..... carrot and cucumber
..... carrot and orange
..... carrot, spinach, celery.

Diluted vegetable juices are also refreshing with whole or
crushed ice cubes and a few suitably chopped herbs – mint,
chives, parsley, fresh sweet basil.

Other combinations: (per person)

Blend with 1 cup of iced water:

. . . . . 2 lightly steamed carrots, 2 slices of fresh pineapple.
         (Steaming carrots makes the vitamin A more readily
         available.)
. . . . . 1 apple, 2 lightly steamed carrots, 1 stick of celery.
. . . . . 2 lightly steamed florets of broccoli, 1 pear.

Barley Water

                         (makes approx. 3 pt, 1.7 litres, 8 cups)
Preparation time 1½ hours

  4 tbsp pot barley (organic)
  8 cups water
  juice and rind of 2 oranges (unsprayed or organic)
  juice and rind of 2 lemons (unsprayed or organic)
  raw honey (optional)

Rinse the barley. Place the barley and the water into a
saucepan. Bring to the boil and then simmer for about an
hour. Wash the fruit thoroughly, squeeze the juice into a jug,
cut the rinds into strips and put those in too. Strain the
barley water into the jug onto the strips of rind and leave to
cool. Strain again to remove the fruit skins. Sweeten with
honey (optional). Store in the fridge.

13

SWEET TREATS

When I first began to change our eating pattern I found providing alternatives to the popular sweets, cakes and biscuits very difficult. As a result I simply didn't offer any. As the children were still very young this did not bring any complaints. However, once they went to primary school, they began to comment and request snacks other than pieces of fruit or nuts and dried fruit.

We now have quite a repertoire but like any treat they are not consumed daily. They are nevertheless wholefoods as well as being great sources of energy.

BISCUITS AND COOKIES

Basic Biscuit Dough
We use our oil pastry recipe (p. 70) as our base for many biscuits and vary our choice of flours – gram flour, maizemeal and soya flour are particularly useful, and you can even substitute ground almonds. It does not take much imagination if you have a good store cupboard to create variations on a theme by using nuts, seeds, dried fruits, carob and pure essences in combination with the basic dough. Other specific recipes follow.

Orange Biscuits
Preparation time 50 mins.   *(approx. 20 biscuits)*

2 fl oz (55ml, ¼ cup) cold-pressed corn oil
3 level tbsp frozen orange juice concentrate

½ tsp pure orange oil
1 egg, free-range and organic preferably
8 oz (225g, 1⅓ cups) wholewheat flour, organic
3 oz (85g, ½ cup) sultanas (unsulphured, washed, dried)
ghee

Combine the corn oil, orange concentrate, orange oil and
egg and beat well together. Add the flour and sultanas and
lightly knead to form a soft dough. Cover the dough and
chill it for 30 minutes in the fridge.

Preheat the oven at gas 5 (190°C, 375°F). Lightly grease a
baking tray with ghee. Roll the dough out thinly on a floured
board and cut into biscuit-shapes. Bake for 10–15 minutes or
until a golden colour. Cool on a wire tray and store in an
airtight container.

Fresh Ginger Snaps
Preparation time 50 mins.   *(approx. 20 snaps)*

3 fl oz (75ml, ⅓ cup) cold-pressed sunflower oil
2 tbsp malt
2 heaped tsp fresh, grated ginger
8 oz (225g, 1⅓ cups) wholewheat flour, organic
3–4 tbsp chilled water and lemon juice to bind
ghee

Measure the oil and the malt into a saucepan using an oiled
spoon to avoid a sticky mess when measuring the malt.
Warm slightly to a pouring consistency. Alternatively, blend
in a food processor. Grate the ginger into the flour and then
fork in the malt and oil mixture. Slowly add the water and
lemon juice to form a soft dough. Cover the bowl or put the
dough in a polythene bag and refrigerate for half an hour.

Preheat the oven at gas 5 (190°C, 375°F). Grease a baking
tray lightly with ghee. Roll the chilled dough out thinly on a
floured board and cut into shapes. Bake the ginger snaps for
5–10 minutes until golden. Cool on a wire tray and store in
an airtight container.

Crunchy Peanut Butter Twigs
Preparation time 45 mins.   *(approx. 48 twiglets)*

2 fl oz (55ml, ¼ cup) cold-pressed corn oil
2 level tbsp malt
1 heaped tbsp crunchy peanut butter (sugar- and salt-
   free)
1 egg, free-range and organic preferably
8 oz (225g, 1⅓ cups) wholewheat flour, organic
2 tsp baking powder (p. 146)
ghee

Measure the oil and malt into a pan (use an oiled spoon so
the malt doesn't stick to it) and warm slightly while you mix
them. Alternatively, blend in a food processor. Add the
peanut butter and egg and mix well. Combine the flour and
baking powder with the wet mixture to form a soft tacky
dough. Chill in the fridge for about 20 minutes.

Preheat the oven at gas 5 (190°C, 375°F). Break off small
pieces of the dough and roll each between your fingers into
twig shapes. Place on a baking tray greased with ghee and
cook for 15 minutes. Cool on a wire tray and then store in an
airtight container.

Fig or Date Clusters
Preparation time 25 mins.   *(approx. 25–30 clusters)*

ghee
4 tbsp cold-pressed sunflower oil
2 tbsp malt or rice syrup
2 tbsp water
1 egg, free-range and organic
1 tsp vanilla essence or 1 tbsp vanilla extract
4 oz (110g, 1 cup) brown rice flour
4 oz (110g, ¾ cup) maizemeal
½ tsp cinnamon
4 oz (110g, 1 cup) dried figs (or dates), chopped

Preheat the oven at gas 5 (190°C, 375°F). Grease a baking
tray with ghee. Combine thoroughly all the wet ingredients

in a mixing bowl or processor. Now mix in all the dry ingredients (except the fruit if you are using a processor) with the wet ones. Press together to form a soft dough. Add the chopped fruit if you haven't already and distribute it evenly. Drop by spoonfuls onto the prepared baking tray and cook for 15–20 minutes until the tips become golden. Cool on a wire tray and store in an airtight container.

Lulu's Banana Cookies
Preparation time 35 mins.   *(approx. 24 cookies)*

3 ripe bananas
4 tbsp cold-pressed sunflower oil
1 tsp vanilla essence or 1 tbsp vanilla extract (p. 147)
handful of chopped dates or figs
2 oz (55g, 1/4 cup) chopped walnuts or sunflower seeds
8 oz (225g, 2 2/3 cups approx.) organic oats

Preheat the oven at gas 4 (180°C, 350°F). Mash the bananas and beat with the oil and vanilla. Add the remaining ingredients and mix well. Allow the mixture to stand for 5 minutes so that the oats can absorb the oil mixture. Drop spoonfuls of the mixture onto an ungreased baking sheet and cook for 25 minutes. Cool and store in an airtight container in the fridge. They freeze well.

This recipe also makes a delicious flan base topped with whipped banana ice cream and frozen blackberries.

"SWEETMEATS"

Sweetmeats are great in lunch boxes as they are a terrific energy source. They also make delicious presents if arranged in gift boxes. A food processor makes light work of the grinding and chopping. Use any cup as your measure but keep the same one throughout a recipe – the exact amounts aren't important.

Fig Balls

There are endless variations you can make with other dried fruits. Substitute orange juice and peel too in place of the lemon if you wish.

Preparation time 10–15 mins.   *(makes about 20)*

3/4 **cup dried figs**
1/2 **cup raw peanuts**
1 tsp lemon juice
1 tsp grated lemon peel (only if the lemon is unsprayed
    or organic)
sesame seeds, wheatgerm or coconut

Wash and dry the figs. Either chop or process them. Combine them with the nuts, lemon juice and peel and mix well. Form small balls and coat them lightly in sesame seeds, wheatgerm or coconut. Store in the fridge or freeze.

Spice Balls

Preparation time 10–15 mins.   *(makes approx. 20)*

1 handful of dates
1 handful of figs
3 tsp frozen orange juice concentrate
1/2 **tsp ground cardamom seeds**
unsweetened, desiccated coconut

Wash, dry and either finely chop or process the fruits. Add the juice and the ground cardamom seeds. Mix to form a dough. Form into small balls and roll them in coconut. Store in the fridge or freezer.

Apricot Treats

Preparation time 10–15 mins.   *(makes 20–30)*

3/4 **cup apricots, unsulphured**
3/4 **cup ground almonds**
2 tbsp desiccated coconut, unsweetened
1 tsp fresh lemon juice

1 tsp fresh orange juice
1 tsp lemon rind (only if unsprayed or organic)
wheatgerm

Wash the apricots and soak them overnight or alternatively
steam them for 5 minutes. Drain well. Process or finely chop
them and then add the almonds, coconut, juices and lemon
rind. Form into small balls and roll them in the wheatgerm.
Store in the fridge or freezer.

Carob Mint Bars
Preparation time 15–20 mins.   *(makes 15 bars)*

8 oz (225g, 1½ cups) dates
8 oz (225g, 1½ cups) figs
1 tbsp carob powder
2–4 drops of pure peppermint oil
ground sesame seeds

Wash and dry the fruits. Process or finely chop them and
combine them with the carob powder and peppermint oil.
Sprinkle some ground sesame seeds over the base of a baking
tray and press the mixture firmly down with your hands, and
evenly over the whole tray. Sprinkle a little more ground
sesame seeds over the top and press that into the mixture.
Refrigerate. Cut into bars and store in an airtight container
in the fridge or freezer.

Carob Nut Snacks
Preparation time 10–15 mins.   *(makes about 20)*

½ cup peanut butter, salt- and sugar-free
¼ cup carob powder
1 tbsp pure apple juice concentrate
½ cup ground sunflower seeds
½ cup sesame seeds
1 tbsp pumpkin seeds

Combine all the ingredients, mix well, shape and refrigerate
or freeze.

Raisin Rolls
Preparation time 10–15 mins.   *(makes about 20)*

1 cup raisins, untreated
1 cup peanut butter, salt- and sugar-free
1 tsp pure vanilla essence or 1 tbsp vanilla extract (p. 147)
1–2 tbsp raw honey
unsweetened desiccated coconut

Wash, dry and finely chop or process the raisins. Mix with
the peanut butter, vanilla and honey. Roll into log shapes
and coat with coconut. Chill and store in the fridge or
freezer.

Soft Toffees
Malt hardens as it cools down after heating, and mixed in the
ratio 1 part malt to 1½ parts soya flour with just a little
flavouring (2 tsp vanilla essence) makes delicious soft toffee.

Heat the malt until it becomes thin, add the other
ingredients and cook together over a moderate heat. Stir
constantly. Bring the mixture to the boil and simmer for 5
minutes. The mixture will be thick. Remove from the heat,
cool and, with wet hands, shape small toffees.

Variations can be achieved by adding a little carob and a
few chopped walnuts or perhaps a little coconut, or a few
chopped raisins and almonds – add as much as you like. Rice
syrup is an alternative to malt.

Candied Peel
When you make your own candied peel try to buy unsprayed
oranges, lemons, grapefruits and limes as commercial grade
citrus fruits are heavily treated.

If you cannot find unsprayed or organic fruit then the best
you can do is to scrub the skins hard in 1 part vinegar to 8
parts water. Rinse them in fresh water and towel dry.

selection of citrus fruits
diluted apple juice concentrate (half juice to half water)

Peel a selection of citrus fruits, put the skins on a chopping board and keep the fruit in a covered container in the fridge, for a fruit salad. Cut the peel into strips and then cut cross-wise into very small pieces. Place in a saucepan, add sufficient diluted fruit juice to cover the cut peel, bring to the boil and then simmer until all the liquid has evaporated, stirring from time to time. Chill and store in a screw-top jar in the fridge. Keeps well.

GLOSSARY OF INGREDIENTS

Agar-agar (kanten) is a seaweed and an excellent vegetarian gelling agent. Use 2 tsp powder to each pint of liquid or 1 tbsp flakes to every 2 pints of liquid. Boil for 5 minutes.

Arrowroot is a tasteless thickening agent extracted from a tropical plant. 2 tsp will thicken 1 pint of liquid. First mix to a paste, add the liquid, bring to the boil and then simmer for 3 minutes.

Buckwheat is related to the rhubarb family and is not a wheat. It is rich in iron and can be cooked like millet. Toast raw buckwheat in a greased and heated pan, add boiling water (1 cup buckwheat to 2 cups boiling water), cover with a tightly fitting lid wrapped in a cloth and secured tightly at the top to prevent fire risk, lower the heat and leave until all the water has been absorbed – about 30 minutes.

Carob is a nutritious alternative to cocoa. It is naturally sweeter than cocoa and is free of caffeine. It is high in calcium. (Cocoa contains oxalic acid which can lock up calcium, thereby making it unavailable to the body.) Carob is known to be a bowel conditioner and an aid to digestive troubles as it contains pectin. It comes from the locust tree, and the pods and seeds are known as St. John's Bread. Use the flour or powder in place of cocoa and, as it is naturally sweet, reduce the amount of any added sweetener.

Gluten is the stretchy remains of wheat dough after all the starch has been washed off. **Seitan** is gluten which has been boiled with oil, soy sauce and seasoning. Use in casseroles, on kebabs and barbecues. It can be bought in healthfood shops.

Hunza apricots are small, unsulphured apricots which are a staple part of the diet of the Hunza people who live long and very healthy lives high up in the Himalayas. The apricots are rich in iron and the kernels taste like almonds – eat no more than four per day.

Miso is a savoury paste made from fermented soya beans with added sea salt. The dark miso contains more soya and more salt than the light miso which contains wheat and less salt. Use in place of yeast extract but do not boil as the beneficial enzymes are killed at high temperatures.

Quark is a hung yoghurt cheese available from supermarkets.

Sea vegetables – kelp, arame, kombu, nori, spirulina, wakame – are all sources of iodine, other trace minerals and proteins. They add a natural saltiness to foods.

Seitan – see Gluten.

Tahini is a paste made by grinding sesame seeds and is a particularly good source of calcium. Use as a spread, in creamy desserts or as a binder in "burger" type mixtures – 1 tbsp will replace an egg.

Tamari is a sauce made from fermenting soya beans with added sea salt. **Shoyu** is another soy sauce but it is made from a combination of soya and wheat.

Tempeh is a highly flavoured convenience food for vegetarians. It is another product of fermented soya beans and provides complete protein and vitamin B_{12}. A little goes a long way!

Tofu (soya bean curd) is a superior plant protein which we often use raw or cooked. It can even be frozen (see below), then thawed and cooked. After freezing and thawing, it has a very different texture from the unfrozen. Soft or silken tofu is best used in creams and sauces, although blended firm tofu does just as well. To freeze firm tofu, make sure you drain off all its liquid before wrapping it tightly in greaseproof paper and in freezer covering, and then freezing.

Vecon – a seaweed-based savoury spread. It may be used as an alternative to a yeast-based spread.

APPENDIX

Useful books for further reference on additives include:
Danger! – Additives At Work (A Report on Food Additives; their use and control) by Melanie Miller, published by The London Food Commission, P.O. Box 291, London N5 1DU.
E For Additives by Maurice Hanssen, published by Thorsons.

Suspected carcinogens listed in *Additives At Work* include E123 Amaranth, E127 Eyrthrosine, 128 Red 2G, 133 Brilliant Blue FCF, E150 Caramels, 154 Brown FK, E230 Diphenyl, E249 – E252 Nitrates and Nitrites, E320 – E321 BHA and BHT, E407 Carrageenan, 430 and 435 Poly-oxyethylene compounds, E466 Sodium Carboxymethyl cellulose, 553 Silicates, 907 Mineral Oils and Waxes, saccharin, Isopropyl Alcohol, Ethyl Acetate.

For further details on protein:
Diet For A Small Planet by Frances Moore Lappe, published by Ballantine Books, New York, is an excellent, informative book for those who wish in-depth information on protein.

For further details on vitamins:
The Vitamin Bible by Earl Mindell, published by Arlington Books, London.
And *Vitamin Vitality* (published by Collins) and *The Whole Health Guide To Elemental Health* (published by Thorsons) both by Patrick Holford are very good reference books should you wish to study the subject in more detail.

INDEX

This index has been compiled to help the wholefood cook, especially the novice. Ingredients, particularly novel ones or ones liable to need being used up, are included, (omitting ones of which only a small amount is used). This is so that if you have some left-over ingredients you can quickly locate recipes in which they might be used. Words in italics refer to actual recipes.

Readers may be interested in the wide range of Paperfronts available. A full
catalogue can be had by sending S.A.E. to the address below.

ELLIOT RIGHT WAY BOOKS,
KINGSWOOD, SURREY, U.K.